Mnemonics

For Psychiatry

David J. Robinson, M.D., F.R.C.P.C.
Diplomate of the American Board
of Psychiatry & Neurology

Rapid Psychler Press

Suite 374
3560 Pine Grove Ave.
Port Huron, Michigan
USA 48060

Suite 203
1673 Richmond St.
London, Ontario
Canada N6G 2N3

Toll Free Phone   888-PSY-CHLE (888-779-2453)
Toll Free Fax   888-PSY-CHLR (888-779-2457)
Outside the U.S. & Canada – Fax 519-675-0610

website   www.psychler.com
email   rapid@psychler.com

ISBN 1-894328-06-X
Printed in the United States of America
© 2001, Rapid Psychler Press
First Edition, First Printing

All caricatures are purely fictitious. Any resemblance to real people, either living or deceased, is entirely coincidental (and unfortunate). The author assumes no responsibility for the consequences of diagnoses made, or treatment instituted, as a result of the contents of this book – such determinations should be made by qualified mental health professionals. Every effort was made to ensure the information in this book was accurate at the time of publication. However, due to the changing nature of the field of psychiatry, the reader is encouraged to consult additional, and more recent, sources of information.

Dedication

To my parents, Monty and Lilly, who, by using Smarties® to help me learn the colors, developed my memory skills at an early age.

Rapid Psychler Press

produces books and presentation media that are:

• comprehensively researched
• well organized
• formatted for ease of use
• reasonably priced
• clinically oriented, and
• include humor that enhances education, and that neither demeans patients nor the efforts of those who treat them

Table of Contents

Author's Foreword

I am an avid collector of Coca-Cola® merchandise, particularly cans from other places. In a dozen years, I have managed to expand my collection to include over 40 different countries. One of the unique items I have comes from Japan. What sets this can apart from all the others is that it comes with instructions detailing how to open the tab. While I have no doubt that most consumers don't need this assistance, someone must have found it helpful. The two-step instructions on this can inspired me to provide a fuller explanation for this text, since its place in psychiatric education may not be obvious to some people.

Mnemonics & More for Psychiatry was written principally to provide medical and allied health science students with a concise, practical handbook to use during psychiatric rotations. It is not a replacement for a standard textbook – this book covers a broad scope of topics, but provides a modest amount of information in these areas.

My suggestion is that this book can be used in two ways:
• As an introduction to psychiatry; by reading this book first, students gain a solid introduction from which to build their knowledge from more detailed texts
• As an aid to "jogging" one's memory for information gleaned from other sources (particularly for exam review)

As a psychiatric educator, I have seldom heard other supervisors say something like "that's all you need to know about this topic." The amount of information required in clinical situations continues to grow exponentially. Textbooks increase in size with each new edition, but what has not progressed as far are ways to organize and recall this information.

I didn't actually use mnemonics as a student – I developed them at the request of the students I've taught. I realize that not everyone is a fan of mnemonic devices. The information included in the mnemonics is valuable, and those not enamored with my creations are certainly free to reorganize the material in any way they see fit. Furthermore, I have included supplemental information beyond the mnemonics (principally in the *Practice Points* Section).

Mnemonics & More for Psychiatry

Where possible, I developed mnemonics that reflect some aspect of the disorder being presented (e.g. 'FEARED' for phobic disorders). I fully realize that some of these mnemonics are better than others – in a number of cases it was difficult to even generate a word from the material (vowels are sometimes hard to come by).

I tried to develop mnemonics that assisted with the most difficult aspects of a topic. For major psychiatric conditions, this is usually the diagnostic criteria from the DSM-IV. A second key area is psychotropic medication. Most students can remember the indications for a medication, but not its side effects, so acrostics were generated for this purpose. It was not my intent to emphasize the side effects of medication over the considerable benefits provided – just to assist with the areas students struggle with the most.

Throughout my studies and my teaching duties, I have found humor to be a most effective and enjoyable way of encouraging learning. For this reason, I have used levity as an educational enhancement in this book. I feel that humor is vital in achieving the balance and perspective that is essential to include in educational material. For example, in the *Personality Disorder* Section, I included caricatures exaggerating some aspects of these conditions. This was not done out of disrespect or disregard for those who suffer from these disorders. Quite the opposite. These conditions are among the most difficult to teach, and I felt that the added visual element aids comprehension, retention, and recall. In this way I hope to promote understanding, and ultimately, tolerance. Additionally, if a book is enjoyable to read, I believe students will have more enthusiasm when reading it, and also retain more of the material.

I am most interested in constructive criticism, and particularly in receiving mnemonics that are an improvement on the ones included here. Please contact me through Rapid Psychler Press (information included on page ii).

Keep Psychling!

Dave Robinson

London, Ontario, Canada
January, 2001

Acknowledgments

I am indebted to the following individuals for their unfailing support and enthusiasm in assisting me with this text.

- **Brian & Fanny Chapman**
- **Monty & Lilly Robinson**
- **Lisa & Cathy Burgard**
- **Brad Groshok**
- **Dean Avola**
- **Dr. Donna Robinson & Dr. Robert Bauer**

I would like to thank the following individuals for their numerous helpful suggestions:

- **Dr. Janine Robertson**
- **Dr. Julia Upton**
- **Tom Norry, B.Sc.N.**
- **Thomas Gantert, B.Sc.N.**
- **Dr. Michelle Kelly**
- **Dr. Sandra Northcott**
- **Dr. Lisa Bogue**
- **Dr. Matt Distefano**

Publication Notes

Terminology

Throughout this book, the term "patient" is used to refer to people who are suffering, and who seek help while bearing pain without complaint or anger.

The terms "consumer" or "consumer-survivor" reflect an unfortunate trend that is pejorative towards mental health care, labeling it as if it were a trade or business instead of a profession. These terms are also ambiguous, as it is not clear what is being "consumed" or "survived."

Graphics

All of the illustrations in this book are original works of art commissioned by Rapid Psychler Press and are a signature feature of our publications.

Rapid Psychler Press makes available an entire library of color illustrations (including those from this book) as 35mm slides, overhead transparencies, and in digital formats (for use in programs such as PowerPoint®). These images are available for viewing and can be purchased from our website — **www.psychler.com**

These images from our color library may be used for presentations.

We request that you respect our copyright and do not reproduce these images in any form, for any purpose, at any time.

Bolded Terms

Throughout this book, various terms appear in bolded text to allow for ease of identification. Many of these terms are defined in this text. Others are only mentioned because a detailed description is beyond the scope of this book. Fuller explanations of all of the bolded terms can be found in standard reference texts.

1. The Diagnosis & Classification of Mental Disorders

Why Is It Important to Make a Diagnosis?

Rather than simply applying a "label" it is crucial to be able to accurately diagnose psychiatric conditions. A diagnosis is a key step in helping patients. After establishing a diagnosis, a management plan develops, involving investigations and treatment for biological, social, and psychological factors. Medical records are legally required to contain a diagnosis, which is used for a variety of statistical purposes. Complete diagnostic assessments are important for funding, research, and clinical initiatives.

How Is a Diagnosis Made?

The assessment process in psychiatry relies primarily on the interviewing and observational skills of practitioners. There is no blood test, X-ray, or single symptom that identifies a psychiatric condition.

There are four components to making an accurate diagnosis:
• The interview
• The mental status exam
• Collateral sources of information
• Laboratory testing

In the **mental status exam (MSE)**, psychiatrists ask about the symptoms of certain conditions that may or may not have been discussed up to that point in an interview. Specific tests of memory, calculation, judgment, etc. are often also included. The MSE is the psychiatric equivalent of the physical exam performed by other doctors.

Collateral sources of information are very important for psychiatrists. This is usually provided by family members, medical records, **primary care providers (PCPs)**, etc.

Psychiatric diagnoses are made in face-to-face interviews. Physical examinations, lab investigations, and other special tests are often arranged in order to exclude the possibility that medical conditions, medications, or recreational drugs are the cause of the psychiatric symptoms. Interestingly, psychiatric conditions can be perfectly imitated by physical illnesses or substance use.

What's Used In Making a Diagnosis?

Signs and symptoms in psychiatry ultimately are subjective, which is probably the single most perplexing aspect for those learning about mental illness. Concepts, definitions, and diagnostic practices vary between practitioners, which is one of the many challenges facing the specialty. For example, the term "schizophrenia" was historically applied to a diverse number of conditions, making research efforts and communication between psychiatrists difficult. In 1952, the **American Psychiatric Association (APA)** published the **Diagnostic and Statistical Manual of Mental Disorders (DSM)** in recognition of the need for standardization. The DSM-II, published in 1968, contained paragraphs describing psychiatric conditions. It was not until the DSM-III was published in 1980 that individual criteria for all psychiatric disorders were clearly set out. The **World Health Organization (WHO)** publishes a similar set of diagnostic criteria called the **International Classification of Diseases**, currently in its tenth edition (**ICD-10**). Greater integration between the DSM and the ICD classification systems is planned for future editions.

The DSM uses five "axes" to completely describe a person's diagnosis and social situation. This **multiaxial approach** to diagnosing mental illness provides clinicians with a method for organizing, recording, and transmitting information. By considering each person's unique set of circumstances, treatment plans can be individualized. It is for this reason that patients with the same diagnosis may well receive different types of treatment.

- **Axis I**: Major Psychiatric Syndromes or Clinical Disorders
- **Axis II**: Personality Disorders, Prominent Maladaptive Personality Features, Ego Defense Mechanisms, and Mental Retardation
- **Axis III**: General Medical Conditions
- **Axis IV**: Psychosocial and Environmental Problems
- **Axis V**: Global Assessment of Functioning (**GAF** Scale which ranges from 1 to 100; 0 is used when there is inadequate information)

Axis I Disorders

The disorders listed on Axis I are the major clinical disorders seen in psychiatry. In order to make the categories listed below more familiar, examples of some of the better known illnesses are included in brackets:

• Psychotic Disorders (e.g. schizophrenia, delusional disorder)
• Mood Disorders (e.g. depression, bipolar disorder)
• Anxiety Disorders (e.g. obsessive-compulsive disorder, phobias)
• Somatoform Disorders (e.g. hypochondriasis, body dysmorphic disorder)
• Factitious Disorders (e.g. "Munchausen" syndrome)
• Dissociative Disorders (e.g. dissociative identity disorder – formerly called multiple personality disorder)
• Sexual and Gender Identity Disorders (e.g. exhibitionism, fetishism)
• Eating Disorders (e.g. anorexia nervosa, bulimia nervosa)
• Sleep Disorders (e.g. narcolepsy, sleep apnea)
• Impulse-Control Disorders (e.g. pathological gambling, kleptomania)
• Adjustment Disorder (excessive emotional reactions to identifiable events or stressors)

Axis II Disorders

Axis II is concerned with aspects usually established by adulthood, and that have an enduring quality. While many Axis I conditions do indeed last a lifetime, some illnesses affect people in an episodic manner. The principal considerations on Axis II are those of adaptability of personality and intellect. Specifically, **personality disorders** (defined as an extreme set of characteristics going beyond the range found in most people) and **mental retardation** (subnormal mental functioning present by the age of 18 years) are the main conditions recorded on Axis II. The DSM also uses Axis II to record prominent **personality traits** and **defense mechanisms**. For example, if a patient meets most, but not all, of the criteria for the paranoid personality disorder, this is recorded as "paranoid personality features." If a personality disorder or strong features are not evident, but the patient uses a defense mechanism to a maladaptive degree, this is recorded as "frequent use of (name of defense)." Other official entries for coding on Axis II can be "no diagnosis" or "diagnosis deferred."

Axis III Disorders

Axis III lists general medical problems. Psychiatrists are always on the alert for physical problems that can either initiate or maintain the symptoms of a mental illness.

Axis IV & V

Symptoms that cause significant distress or impairment in social or occupational functioning (or in other important areas) are considered to be diagnostic criteria. Stressors in day-to-day functioning are recorded on Axis IV. These are:
• Problems with primary support group
• Educational problems
• Occupational problems
• Housing problems
• Economic problems
• Problems with access to health care services
• Problems related to the social environment
• Problems related to interactions with the legal system/crime

Examples of these stressors are listed in the DSM-IV on page 29 (APA, 1994). The **GAF Scale** appears on page 32 (APA, 1994).

Other categories of psychiatric illness listed in the DSM-IV are:
• Disorders Usually First Diagnosed in Infancy, Childhood, or Adolescence (called child psychiatric disorders)
• Delirium, dementia, and other cognitive disorders (while not considered to be mental illnesses, these conditions do cause a number of psychiatric symptoms)
• Substance-Related Disorders (just as with general medical illnesses, screening for substance-related disorders is imperative because they can mimic almost any psychiatric condition)

The DSM-IV also lists severity specifiers for psychiatric conditions (described below).

Severity Specifiers for Psychiatric Conditions
• **Mild:** Few, if any, symptoms in excess of those required to make the diagnosis are present, and symptoms result in no more than minor impairment in social or occupational functioning.

• **Moderate:** Impairment between mild and severe.

• **Severe:** Many symptoms in excess of those required to make the diagnosis, or several symptoms that are particularly severe are present, or the symptoms result in marked impairment in social or occupational functioning.

A Method for Understanding Mental Illness

Sensorium
(level of consciousness, ability to attend to stimuli)

Perceiving
(sight, smell, hearing, touch, and taste)

Thinking
(cognition)

The Environment

(external reality, other people, society, etc.)

Feeling
(emotion)

Behaving
(action)

The schematic shown on the previous page is useful in conceptualizing mental illnesses. Any condition that affects one area will have an effect on all the others. For example, consider depression, which is primarily a disorder of mood that causes people to feel sad, blue, or empty. The effects that a depressed mood causes can be illustrated as follows:

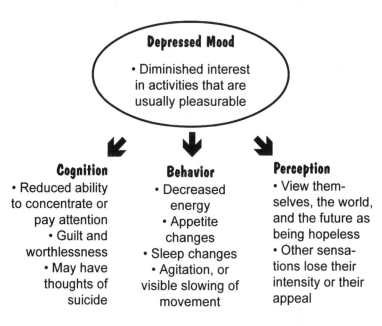

Depressed Mood

- Diminished interest in activities that are usually pleasurable

Cognition
- Reduced ability to concentrate or pay attention
- Guilt and worthlessness
- May have thoughts of suicide

Behavior
- Decreased energy
- Appetite changes
- Sleep changes
- Agitation, or visible slowing of movement

Perception
- View themselves, the world, and the future as being hopeless
- Other sensations lose their intensity or their appeal

The majority of the criteria used to diagnose mental illness in the DSM-IV can be categorized as being changes in perception, cognition, emotion, or behavior. Though an oversimplification, many types of treatment can be viewed as assisting primarily with one of these four areas, which in turn will have a beneficial effect on the other aspects of mental functioning. For example:

Area	Type of Treatment
Perception	Medication
Cognition	Cognitive Therapy; Rational-Emotive Therapy
Emotion	Psychodynamic Therapies; Medication
Behavior	Behavior Therapy; Behavior Modification

Psychiatry as a Medical Specialty

Psychiatry is a fascinating, and at times frustrating, field for both students and practitioners.

Psychiatry is fascinating because it deals with the most basic of human problems – emotion, perception, cognition, and behavior. Treating mental illness provides the practitioner with perpetual variety because it involves the most complicated entity in the known universe (the human brain, not managed care). Whereas most cases of congestive heart failure or glaucoma have set treatment protocols, psychiatric illnesses require creative interventions.

Psychiatry is frustrating in that the pathognomonic findings or objective signs found in physical medicine are no longer present. No single sign or symptom is unique to a particular psychiatric diagnosis. We cannot rely on a blood test, MRI, or laparoscopy to clear up diagnostic uncertainty. Substance abuse can perfectly mimic any psychiatric condition so that only time and abstinence help to make the distinction. It is also not possible to isolate the illness from psychological or social factors. A surgical patient, for example, is not likely to be kept in hospital longer because of concomitant depression, but this would quite likely occur on a psychiatric ward.

Psychiatry is an all-encompassing field. Every patient on every service experiences an emotional reaction to his or her illness. Convincing a patient to take medications, minimize risk factors, and comply with discharge arrangements involves a multi-faceted understanding of human nature.

The exploration of the cause and effect of illness along the "mind-body continuum" is an area still in its infancy. For example, the interplay between emotions and changes in immune and endocrine function is now an established psychiatric subspecialty.

Psychological factors clearly have an effect on medical conditions, and an understanding of this association helps not only to make us better clinicians (in any field), but better students, teachers, spouses, parents, and indeed, human beings. Despite its current drawbacks and limitations, psychiatry provides a rich and varied approach to understanding and treating mental illness.

2. The Psychiatric Interview

Functions of the Interview

The interview can be defined as "the skill of encouraging disclosure of personal information for a specific professional purpose" (McCready, 1986), and serves a variety of functions:
• Collecting clinical information in an efficient manner
• Eliciting emotions, feelings, and attitudes
• Establishing a doctor-patient relationship and developing rapport
• Generating and testing a set of hypotheses to arrive at a **preferred diagnosis**, accompanied by a list of other conditions (called a **differential diagnosis**) which must be considered
• Determining areas for further investigation
• Developing a treatment plan

Interviewers must develop an understanding (often called a **formulation**) of two main areas, **nosologic** and **dynamic**. Nosologic refers to the exercise of figuring out which condition(s) the patient suffers from. The dynamic domain focuses on the biopsychosocial aspects of a patient's illness:
• In what way(s) was the patient **predisposed** to developing this condition?
• What **precipitating** factors caused the illness to emerge at a certain point in time?
• What factors **perpetuate** this illness in its current form?
• What **protective factors** (strengths, supports, resources, etc.) does this patient have?

Often, these parameters are divided into biological, social, and psychological components. A grid can be constructed to aid the process of dynamic formulation:

	Biological	Social	Psychological
Predisposing			
Precipitating			
Perpetuating			
Protective			

Anatomy of the Psychiatric Interview

The American Psychiatric Association (2000) published a set of practice guidelines for general psychiatric evaluation of adults. The following "domains of evaluation" comprise a complete psychiatric interview:

A. Reason for the Evaluation
B. History of the Present Illness
C. Past Psychiatric History
D. General Medical History
E. History of Substance Use
F. Psychosocial/Developmental History (Personal History)
G. Social History
H. Occupational History
 I. Family History
J. Review of Symptoms
K. Physical Examination
L. Mental Status Examination (MSE)
M. Functional Assessment
N. Diagnostic Tests
O. Information Derived From The Interview Process

A modified approach to the interview is outlined on pages 12 – 18.

Identifying Features (ID)

Identifying features are a patient's demographics, and help build a mental picture of that person's unique social makeup. While this information is the first to be included in verbal and written presentations of case material, it is a matter of style as to when it is obtained. Some clinicians advocate a period of "small talk" prior to formally beginning the interview. If this can be done naturally, it is a nice way to ease into the assessment. As an alternative, "icebreaker" questions can be asked about the patient's identifying features:
• Name
• Age
• Gender
• Cultural Factors (including race and religion)
• Marital & Parental Status
• Occupational Status

Reason for Evaluation (RFE) or Reason for Referral (RFR)

In most situations, patients access psychiatric care after some type of screening process. In hospital settings, an assessment by an emergency physician or PCP is the most common source of psychiatric referrals. In an emergency department, patients are asked to state the reason for their visit. Their replies are often recorded verbatim on the emergency chart. Similarly, referral letters from other sources frequently include a particular question to be addressed. The RFE/RFR is also called the **Chief Complaint (CC)** or **Presenting Complaint (PC)**.

History of Present Illness (HPI)

The HPI is regarded by many psychiatrists as the most important part of the interview. Some would argue that the MSE is perhaps more important, though at least half (and often more) of the MSE can be obtained in the HPI. The HPI is typically the section that takes the most time to complete.

Goals for the HPI
• Develop rapport
• Keep track of, and investigate, symptoms
• Generate and revise diagnostic hypotheses
• Record at least half of the MSE
• Keep track of cues for further exploration of facts and feelings

Past Psychiatric History (PPH)

Once the HPI is completed, the next section of the interview focuses on developing an understanding of the patient's psychiatric difficulties across his or her entire lifespan. This section is the Psychiatric History, and is often referred to as the **Past Psychiatric History** (even though this is redundant – all history is in the past), abbreviated as **PPH**.

Goals for the PPH
• Construct a time line for the patient's illness (see page 16)
• Determine the course and severity of the disorder
• Formulate an understanding of the predisposing, precipitating, perpetuating, and protective factors affecting the person
• Obtain information about hospitalizations
• Get the details about which treatments have been tried and their effectiveness (for psychotherapy and medication)
• Assess insight and judgment

Medical History (MedHx)

The ability to distinguish between a medical (sometimes called organic) and a psychiatric disorder is widely considered to be the most important skill for a psychiatrist. The ability to make this distinction is so important that a subspecialty of psychiatry, called **Consultation-Liaison (C-L)**, focuses on the interface between medical and psychiatric disorders (see Chapter 14, p. 214). Furthermore, this is why psychiatrists must complete general medical training before embarking on specialty training. The MedHx is the section of the interview where inquiries are made about the presence of physical problems and the treatment being given for such conditions.

Goals for the MedHx
• Enumerate the patient's medical and surgical illnesses
• Ascertain which illnesses are currently active, and determine the course and severity of these conditions
• Get a list of the patient's medications
• Ask about allergies, reactions to medications, side effects, and if the person wears a MedicAlert® bracelet or chain
• Screen for medical conditions that are of particular relevance to psychiatry, and if time permits, conduct a general medical review of systems

Substance Use History (SubHx)

The **history of psychoactive substance use (SubHx)** is a crucial area to ask about in interviews. The DSM-IV criteria for most major clinical disorders contains an exclusionary statement that a diagnosis cannot be made if symptoms are due to the effects of a substance or a general medical condition. Clinicians vary in their opinions on how long a period of abstinence is required before psychiatric symptoms can be considered as due to a primary illness instead of a substance use. The DSM-IV considers early remission to begin one month after the time that no criteria are met for **substance abuse** or **dependence** (see page 200).

Goals for the SubHx
• Determine the consumption pattern of psychoactive substances
• Screen for the presence of substance misuse
• Screen for substances that are impairing social or occupational functioning, causing medical, legal, or psychological problems, and obtain information about the following parameters of use:

"DRAPE"

Duration of use
Route (inhaled, ingested, snorted, injected, etc.)
Amount
Pattern of use (binge, daily, solitary, etc.)
Effects (direct, secondary, adverse, etc.)

Family History (FamHx)

The FamHx and PersHx are very helpful in establishing the psychosocial factors that have shaped patients' lives.

Goals for the FamHx
• Generate a list of immediate family members and obtain key psychosocial information about each of them
• Create a genogram/pedigree (optional)
• Catalog the presence of mental illness in the extended family
• Determine if there are psychiatric illnesses that cluster in family members to whom patients are genetically related
• Determine if neurologic or serious medical illnesses cluster in family members to whom patients are genetically related

Personal History (PersHx)

The PersHx focuses on psychosocial development and the patient's adaptation to social and occupational roles (e.g. as a member of a family, a member of society in general, etc.). The FamHx can record information about the patient's family of origin. The PersHx collects information about the patient's development, first as part of a family, and then in areas of individuation. Clearly, there are areas of overlap between the PersHx and FamHx, and many topics can easily be shifted between these two sections according to an interviewer's style, patient's replies, level of interest, etc.

Goals for the PersHx
• Developmental History
• Child & Adolescent Psychiatric Disorders
• Social & Sexual History
• Abuse History
• Legal History
• Military History
• Obstetrical History
• Occupational/Educational History

Review of Symptoms (ROS)

The ROS can take place almost anywhere in the interview. One advantage of taking it at the end of the PersHx is that you end up discussing current symptoms and stressors, so a smooth transition can be made to the ROS.

Goals for the ROS
The ROS is a search for current symptoms that have not already been identified in the HPI or other areas of the interview. This allows you to accomplish four goals:
• Further refine your hypothesis generation and testing
• Screen for the presence of other conditions that are not the focus of the patient's visit (e.g. phobias, dysthymia, etc.)
• Ask about symptoms of illnesses for which the patient is known to be at particular risk of developing because of historical, genetic, environmental, or demographic factors elicited during the course of the interview
• Conduct a medical review of systems to further delineate general medical conditions, particularly those that can initiate or perpetuate a psychiatric illness

Developing a Time Line

The reference point that separates the HPI from the PPH can be established by asking a question similar to one of the following:
• *When were you last well (or your usual self)?*
• *At what point in time did things change for you?*

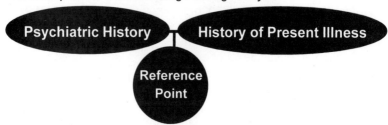

The reference point can also be determined by listening for, or asking about, a precipitant for the patient's current problems, such as:
• Disturbances in interpersonal relationships
• Substance use (e.g. intoxication or withdrawal states)
• Starting or stopping medications for medical or psychiatric illnesses
• Onset of a medical condition

Completing the Time Line

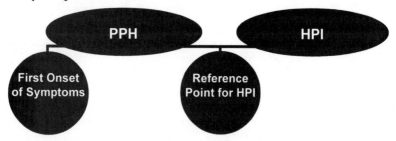

In the PPH, the focus shifts to the duration of the patient's illness. Using the time line developed for the HPI, the emphasis in the PPH is on events leading up to the reference point. The PPH can be obtained in chronological order, with emphasis on the following:
• Age of onset
• Level of functioning prior to the onset of the illness
• Level of functioning between episodes of the illness
• Number of episodes of the illness
• Number of hospitalizations (which can be used as one indicator of the severity of the illness)

Plotting the Course of an Illness

Information can be plotted on a simple graph. The 'Y' axis can represent the presence of symptoms (e.g. none, some, moderate, severe) or level of functioning (good, fair, poor). The 'X' axis is time and starts with the onset of the first episode of the illness.

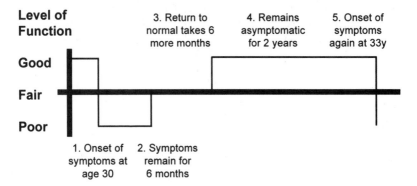

Level of Function

3. Return to normal takes 6 more months

4. Remains asymptomatic for 2 years

5. Onset of symptoms again at 33y

Good

Fair

Poor

1. Onset of symptoms at age 30

2. Symptoms remain for 6 months

On page 10, the **biopsychosocial approach** to understanding psychiatric illness was introduced, complete with a grid. An example of information from the PPH listed in grid form for a patient suffering from depression is as follows:

	Biological	Social	Psychological
Predisposing	family members with depression	awkward and shy around others	loss of mother when patient was age 9 years
Precipitating	use of street drugs (cocaine and amphetamines)	break-up of long-term relationship	failed college exams; has had academic problems before
Perpetuating	unrecognized hypothyroidism	few friends or social supports available	low self esteem; reluctant to attempt courses again
Protective	good general health; will now avoid the use of street drugs	has Employee Assistance Program available through work	above-average intelligence; diversified interests

The course of the illness can be illustrated as on the previous page. Individual episodes can be described as follows:

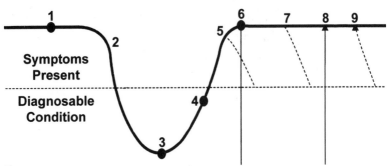

Key

1. Period of normal or usual functioning
2. **Onset** of symptoms
3. Condition is at its most severe; treatment is sought
4. **Response** to treatment occurs
5. **Remission** – a return of symptoms or increase in symptom severity before a complete recovery from the illness
6. **Recovery** – a return to the premorbid level of functioning
7. **Relapse** – a return of symptoms or increase in symptom severity after there has been complete recovery from the illness
8. Continuation of recovery – an arbitrarily defined period of time, often from six months to one year, where various forms of treatment may be discontinued
9. **Recurrence** – a completely new episode of the illness

3. The Mental Status Exam

The Mental Status Exam (MSE)

The mental status exam is the interview component in which cognitive functions are tested and inquiries are made about the symptoms of psychiatric conditions. It is a set of standardized observations and questions designed to evaluate five areas (shown at left).

- Sensorium

- Perception

- Thinking

- Feeling

- Behavior

The MSE is an integral part of *any* clinical interview, not just one that takes place in a psychiatric context. An assessment of cognitive functioning must be made before information from patients can be considered accurate. *The MSE records only observed behavior, cognitive abilities, and inner experiences expressed during the interview.* The MSE is conducted to assess as completely as possible the factors necessary to arrive at a provisional diagnosis, formulate a treatment plan, and follow the clinical course.

The MSE is a portable assessment tool that helps identify psychiatric symptoms and gauge their severity. With experience, it is a specific, sensitive, and inexpensive diagnostic instrument. The MSE takes only a few minutes to administer yet yields information that is crucial to making a diagnostic assessment and starting a course of treatment.

The MSE can be viewed as the equivalent of a physical exam in other areas of medicine. A popular approach to a systematic examination follows the acronym **I.P.P.A.**

- Inspection

- Palpation

- Percussion

- Auscultation

Further "looking into," "touching on," "sounding out," and "listening to," is required to fully evaluate psychiatric symptoms. Both the physical exam and MSE are recorded separately from the body of the history. However, unlike the physical exam, the MSE is at least partly integrated with the history.

Components of the MSE

The MSE can also be thought of as a psychiatric "review of symptoms." The assessment of five main areas yields information necessary for a differential diagnosis and treatment plan. Expanding these five areas gives the psychological functions that are assessed and recorded in the MSE.

Sensorium & Cognitive Functioning

Level of consciousness and attentiveness
Orientation to person, place, and time
Attention
Concentration
Memory
Knowledge
Intelligence
Capacity for abstract thinking

Perception

Disorders of sensory input where there is no stimulus (hallucinations) or where a stimulus is misperceived (illusions), or of disorders of bodily experience (depersonalization or derealization)

Thinking

Speech
Thought Content (*what* is said)
Thought Form (*how* it is said or *the way* it is said)
Suicidal or Homicidal Ideation
Insight & Judgment

Feeling

Affect (objective, visible emotional state)
Mood (subjective emotional experience)

Behavior

Appearance
Psychomotor agitation or retardation
Degree of cooperation with the interview

Components of the MSE

"ABC STAMP LICKER"

Appearance
Behavior
Cooperation

Speech
Thought – **form** and **content**
Affect – visible moment-to-moment variation in emotion
Mood – subjective emotional tone throughout the interview
Perception – in all sensory modalities

Level of consciousness
Insight & Judgment
Cognitive functioning & Sensorium
       Orientation
       Memory
       Attention & Concentration
       Reading & Writing
Knowledge base
Endings – suicidal and/or homicidal ideation
Reliability of the information supplied

Practice Points
• The MSE can also be considered part of the **objective** portion of the **S.O.A.P.** method of recording information:

Subjective – Consists of sections from the interview: Chief Complaint; History of Present Illness; Past History (Medical & Psychiatric); Family and Personal History

Objective – MSE, Physical Examination, Laboratory Testing

Assessment – Provisional Diagnosis & Differential Diagnoses

Plan – Further Investigations, Short and Longer-Term Treatment

More on the MSE

The MSE is often unpopular for two reasons:
• The questions are difficult to formulate because they are not asked in other types of interviews or in other areas of medicine, psychology, nursing, etc.
• The questions appear to be of dubious relevance.

Once these two difficulties are surmounted, the MSE becomes an enjoyable and interesting aspect of interviewing. To achieve this level of comfort, it helps to realize that almost half of the MSE is obtained "free" through observation and discussion from the initial parts of the interview.

"Free" Parameters	Parameters to Ask About
Level of Consciousness	Orientation
Appearance	Cognitive Functioning
Behavior	Suicidal/Homicidal Thoughts
Cooperation	Knowledge Base
Reliability	Perception
Affect	Mood
Thought Form	Thought Content

Remember, all psychiatric diagnoses are made clinically in interview situations. There is no test or single identifying feature for psychiatric conditions. This emphasizes the necessity for a thorough assessment, of which the MSE is an essential component. A sample MSE report is included in Chapter 18 (p. 258).

Practice Points
• The **Mini-Mental State Examination** (**MMSE**) is *NOT* the same as a complete MSE. The MMSE is used to screen for cognitive impairment and does not include several key areas of evaluation (see Chapter 16, p. 231)
• The MSE consists of a relatively standardized approach and set of inquiries. However, an instructor may have his or her own rationale for doing things a certain way. After getting exposure to as many styles as possible, assimilate this knowledge into an approach that suits you. Different approaches can be used at different times in different ways; there is no one "right" approach.

Integration of the MSE and History

Psychiatric History	MSE Component
• Identifying Data • Chief Complaint	• Appearance • Behavior • Orientation (ask patients for their full name, if they had difficulty finding the room/clinic/hospital) • Level of Consciousness (this is usually obvious)
• History of Present Illness (HPI) 5 – 10 minutes of relatively unstructured questions using open-ended inquiries and other facilitating techniques	• Cooperation • Speech • Thought Form • Thought Content (this open format allows patients to talk about what concerns them, a valuable indicator of thought content)
• Exploration of Symptoms from the HPI More focused assessment with elaboration of material from the HPI using closed-ended questions to get more specific information	• Affect • Mood • Suicidal/Homicidal Ideation • Elements of Cognitive Testing (it may be convenient to include these components at this point to help gauge the severity of reported symptoms)

Direct Testing of other MSE Components
If certain areas aren't amenable to questions earlier in the interview, specific inquiries must be made at some point to assess these functions
	• General Knowledge
	• Perception
	• Insight & Judgment
	• Formal Cognitive Testing
	    Memory
	    Attention & Concentration
	    Reading & Writing
	    Abstract Thinking

4. The Psychiatric Physical Exam

Feature

Possible Implications*

Head and Neck
- altered pupil size — drug intoxication/withdrawal
- Argyll Robertson pupil — neurosyphilis
- corneal pigmentation — Wilson's disease
- piercing of lips, nose, eyebrows, etc. — borderline or antisocial personality
- neck mass — thyroid dysfunction
- dental caries — eating disorders (from vomiting)
- nasal septal defect — cocaine use
- arcus senilis — alcohol use
- parotid enlargement — anorexia/bulimia nervosa
- esophagitis — eating disorder (from vomiting)

Skin
- tattoos — borderline or antisocial personality
- callus/laceration on knuckles — eating disorder (due to self-induced vomiting)
- scars from slashing — borderline personality disorder
- scars from trauma — antisocial personality; alcohol use
- needle marks/tracks — IV drug use
- piloerection — opioid withdrawal
- palmar erythema — alcohol use
- bruising — alcohol use; seizure disorders
- cigarette burns — dementia; alcohol use; other neurologic conditions; self harm
- dermatitis or excoriated skin — OCD – compulsive hand washing; may occur on knees from cleaning in a kneeling position
- unusual pattern of hair loss — trichotillomania
- pretibial myxedema — Graves' disease
- Kaposi's sarcoma — AIDS; HIV encephalopathy
- lanugo hair — anorexia nervosa
- café au lait macules — Neurofibromatosis
- red-purple striae — Cushing's syndrome/disease
- edema — MAOI drugs, anorexia nervosa
- spider angiomata — alcohol use disorder

Cardiovascular
- mitral valve prolapse   anorexia nervosa
- hypotension   anorexia nervosa

Abdomen and Chest
- enlarged liver   alcohol use disorder
- gynecomastia   alcohol use disorder
- dilated abdominal veins   alcohol use disorder
- decreased motility   pica (with a bezoar), anorexia nervosa

Genitals
- chancre   syphilis (primary)
- mutilation   psychotic disorder; paraphilia, gender identity disorder
- testicular atrophy   alcohol use disorder; anabolic steroid use

Musculoskeletal & Nervous System
- gait abnormalities   normal pressure hydrocephalus; dementia paralytica (syphilis); high stepping gait (syphilis); festinating gait (Parkinson's disease); alcohol use (cerebellar degeneration); Wernicke-Korsakoff syndrome
- tremor   Parkinson's disease; lithium use; caffeine intoxication; alcohol withdrawal; anxiety disorders
- repeated movements   Tourette's disorder; tic disorders; autism; tardive dyskinesia; OCD; mental retardation
- muscle wasting   alcohol use disorder

---

* The implications listed here are speculative. They are not meant to be pejorative or to indicate that diagnostic criteria have been met. Furthermore, other diagnoses need to be considered beyond the ones listed here (e.g. there may be many other reasons beyond trichotillomania for unusual patterns of hair loss).

Medical Complications That Can Result from Psychiatric Disorders

Schizophrenia
• Respiratory disorders and lung cancer from cigarette smoking
• Coronary artery disease due to poor diet, obesity, lack of exercise
• Dental caries from anticholinergic side effects of medication
• Movement disorders can occur even without neuroleptic exposure

Mood Disorders
• Trauma from accidents or fights during manic episodes
• Infections from impaired immune function during depression
• Obesity from hyperphagia or carbohydrate craving during certain types of depressive episodes (seasonal or atypical)

Anxiety Disorders
• Chronic anxiety can cause medical conditions in target organs – gastrointestinal and cardiac systems are most commonly affected

Bulimia Nervosa
• Electrolyte disturbances; dehydration; alkalosis; seizures
• Mallory-Weiss tears due to repeated vomiting
• Intestinal motility disturbances related to use of cathartics
• Parotid gland enlargement

Anorexia Nervosa
• The most worrisome complications are cardiac: arrhythmias, brady-cardia, hypotension, and congestive heart failure
• Reduced thyroid metabolism (causing cold intolerance)
• All blood cell counts can be decreased (pancytopenia)
• Kidney stones; osteoporosis; amenorrhea; hypercortisolemia
• Liver function tests become abnormal; amylase levels increase

Somatoform Disorder, Conversion Disorder, Malingering, Factitious Disorder
• Chronic complaints of illness can result in unnecessary investigations and therapeutic procedures (with their inherent risks)
• Patients are at risk for prescription medication abuse

The Scope of Physical Illness in Psychiatric Patients

Undiagnosed medical illnesses have been found in almost half of some psychiatric populations. Psychiatric symptomatology can be, and often is, the first manifestation of a physical illness (there are almost 100 medical disorders that can present with depressive symptoms). Medical illnesses can be the sole cause of a psychiatric condition, or can worsen the course of psychiatric disorders to a variable extent. Possible mechanisms for this interaction are as follows:

Psychiatric Disorders Affecting Medical Illnesses
• Compliance with treatment may be lessened (e.g. patients may have cognitive deficits that prevent a full understanding of their illness, or may have an indifferent attitude towards treatment)
• Risk factors such as poor diet, lack of exercise, obesity, etc. may be more difficult to control
• Substance abuse is more prevalent among psychiatric patients

Psychiatric Treatment Affecting Medical Illnesses
• Psychiatric medications affect many neurotransmitter systems, which can cause a wide array of potential side effects
• As an example, anticholinergic side effects can worsen glaucoma and cause urinary retention; weight gain can have a detrimental effect on the management of diabetes, etc.

Medical Illnesses Affecting Psychiatric Disorders
• The stress of somatic illnesses can cause relapses or recurrences of some psychiatric illnesses (e.g. a schizophrenic patient developing a psychotic episode due to a prolonged ICU stay)
• Emotional reactions to illness can result in psychiatric disorders (e.g. depression, adjustment disorder, etc.)

Medical Treatment Affecting Psychiatric Conditions
• Treatment of medical conditions can cause some psychiatric illnesses (e.g. steroid-induced psychosis) or worsen pre-existing ones (beta-blockers triggering recurrent depression)
• Medications given for sedation and pain control can adversely affect some patients (e.g. with a pre-existing dependency)

Important Organic Considerations
"TIME WON'T PASS"

Trauma – particularly head injuries and intracranial bleeding
Infections – especially of the CNS
Multiple Sclerosis (MS)
Epilepsy

Wilson's disease – an inherited defect in copper metabolism
Obstruction of CSF – Normal Pressure Hydrocephalus (**NPH**)
Nutritional – e.g. vitamin deficiencies, protein-deficient diets, etc.
Toxic – ingestion of medication, heavy metals, chemicals, etc.

Porphyria, **P**heochromocytoma
Axis of the hypothalamus-pituitary-thyroid-adrenal glands
Space-Occupying Lesions
Substances – especially intoxication and withdrawal states

Practice Points
• A correlation between the onset of psychiatric and medical signs/symptoms is especially important to investigate
• The first episode of a psychotic or mood disorder warrants a complete investigation
• New-onset psychiatric illness in the last half of life often has an organic basis
• There is no single pathognomonic sign or symptom for psychiatric conditions; any of the criteria used to diagnose psychiatric illnesses can be caused by medical conditions
• Auditory hallucinations, and to a lesser extent visual hallucinations, commonly are symptoms of psychiatric illnesses; hallucinations in other senses warrant an investigation for organic causes
• CT scans are indicated for imaging intracranial calcification, cerebral hemorrhages and tumor margins; MRI scans provide superior resolution over CT scans; they are particularly useful for multiple sclerosis and other demyelinating diseases and for imaging the posterior fossa and brain stem
• *"The body can have as many diseases as it pleases"*

Differential Diagnosis of Medical Conditions

"MASTER THIS SCID"

Metabolic
Autoimmune
Septic/Infectious
Traumatic
Endocrine
Renal

Toxic
Hematologic/Circulatory
Idiopathic
Structural

Somatoform (Psychiatric)
Congenital
Iatrogenic
Degenerative

> The SCID stands for the *Structured Clinical Interview for the DSM-IV*

"VITAMIN CDE"

Vascular
Infectious
Traumatic
Autoimmune
Metabolic
Idiopathic
Neoplasm

Congenital
Drug Induced (Iatrogenic)
Endocrine

Overview of the Assessment Process

Standard Interview Process

Mental Status Exam

Physical Exam & Routine Investigations

Specialized Investigations
- Biochemical
- Neuro-imaging
- Other

5. Laboratory Testing

Laboratory Testing

A thorough history and physical examination will detect more medical illnesses than requesting lab tests, particularly when such tests are ordered as part of a routine screening battery, or for "case finding." Unfortunately, there has been considerable debate about the extent to which lab testing can be justified on admission to a psychiatric unit, and clear guidelines have not yet been established.

While some studies revealed abnormalities at a rate of up to 10% for routine screening tests, less than half were deemed to be clinically significant. Many "unexpectedly" abnormal results are not investigated further, and about one-fifth of tests are found to be within normal limits when they are repeated. Overall, only about 20% of abnormal results require further action. Patients with no physical signs or symptoms were found to have a true-positive rate as low as 0.06%.

There are two other factors that need to be considered in determining the extensiveness of screening laboratory tests. First, if the patient appears to be suffering from a severe psychiatric illness (e.g. schizophrenia, mania), an organic work-up is indicated, particularly if the patient cannot provide a reliable history. Second, the first episode of an illness warrants careful scrutiny for physical causes, particularly in older patients.

Rationale for Ordering Laboratory Tests
Tests are indicated if they will:
• Contribute to the diagnosis of a medical disorder that cannot be detected by history or physical exam
• Necessitate a referral to a medical specialist if abnormal
• Influence further management

Tests are not indicated if they:
• Merely confirm an established diagnosis
• Yield results that will be of uncertain diagnostic usefulness

Guidelines for Ordering Laboratory Tests to Detect Physical Illnesses in Psychiatric Patients
Screening tests (which can detect up to 75% of physical illnesses)
• Vital signs   • Glucose

- Urinalysis
- Renal function tests (RFTs)
- Thyroid function tests (TFTs)
- Complete blood count (CBC)
- Liver function tests (LFTs)

Investigations Warranted by Positive Findings in the History or the Physical Exam

- Calcium and Phosphorus
- EEG/sleep deprived EEG
- EKG
- Neuro-imaging
- Urine drug screen
- Chest X-ray
- Electrolytes
- Folate
- Syphilis serology/VDRL
- Vitamin B_{12}

Practice Points

- Medical illnesses often present with psychiatric symptoms
- Similar symptoms can be reported for medical and psychiatric conditions
- Patients are often unaware of the connection between medical illnesses and psychiatric symptoms
- First-onset psychiatric disorders warrant a full investigation, particularly for psychotic and mood disorders
- Most psychiatric conditions start in the first half of life; patients who have the onset of their disorders beyond this period deserve particular attention for organic causes
- Features in a patient's history that are indicative of organic pathology are: alcohol or drug use, disorientation, self-neglect, visual hallucinations or illusions, and complaints of 4 or more physical symptoms
- Psychiatric patients receive a variable degree of medical care, making thorough physical examinations a necessity
- Patients with psychiatric illnesses are at high risk for developing physical illnesses, and these illnesses will impact on the course of their psychiatric problems
- Screening laboratory investigations infrequently uncover illnesses that are not elucidated in the history or have positive findings on physical examination
- More extensive laboratory testing is indicated in patients with unusual presentations of psychiatric illnesses, or who have not responded to treatment
- The most common types of medical conditions causing psychiatric disorders are (in order): Endocrine, Neurologic, Toxic/Withdrawal, and Nutritional/Infectious

6. Evaluating Cognitive Abilities

Memory

Brain areas involved in memory
- Verbal memory   dominant temporal lobe
- Visual memory   non-dominant temporal lobe
- Registration   frontal & temporal lobes
- Short-term memory   hippocampus (consolidation & retrieval); temporal lobe (storage); medial dorsal thalamic nuclei (storage)
- Long-term memory   association cortex of temporal lobe (medial temporal region)

Structures involved in memory
- Hippocampus – has connections to the thalamus and temporal lobe; part of the limbic system
- Amygdala – involved in the integration of memories and the recognition of faces; part of the limbic system
- Mamillary bodies – implicated in the pathology of Korsakoff's syndrome; part of the hypothalamus
- Pulvinar – needed for memory retrieval; part of the thalamus

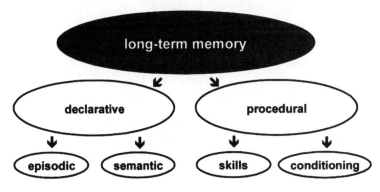

- **Declarative memory** is factual and directly accessible to consciousness. It is also called "knowing that" or "knowing what" memory. *Episodic memory* involves the recall of events and the context in which they occurred (where, when, etc.). *Semantic memory* refers to knowledge not remembered in a specific context.
- **Procedural memory** refers to acquired skills and habits. It is also called "knowing how" memory. This type of memory evolves after many trials, and remains largely intact in various forms of amnesia, unlike declarative memory.

Regional Brain Functions

Frontal Lobe – "LIMP"

Language – Broca's speech area
Intelligence, abstraction
Motor function
Personality variables (e.g. judgment)

Temporal Lobe – "LAME"

Language – Wernicke's speech area
Affective component of speech — prosody
Memory
Emotion

Parietal Lobe – "VAST"

Visuospatial processing
Association areas – integration of sensory input
Symbolic recognition
Topographic sense

Occipital Lobe – "VIP"

Visual **I**ntegration area
Primary visual cortex

Practice Points

retrograde amnesia   **event**   anterograde amnesia

time ⟶

Regional Brain Testing

Frontal Lobe
• Rapid sequential movements
• Complex motor behaviors (e.g. planning, execution)
• Ability to repeat phrases with prosody (executive prosody)
• Problem solving, judgment, concentration, orientation

Temporal Lobe
• Reading
• Writing
• Naming
• Gnosis – recognition of numbers and letters
• Comprehension of spoken language (also receptive prosody)

Parietal Lobe
• Praxis
  • ideomotor – ability to carry out actions on command
  • ideational – ability to carry out acts in a logical sequence
  • constructional – ability to arrange shapes and copy diagrams
• Calculation
• Stereognosis
• Right-left and east-west orientation

Occipital Lobe
• Visual memory
• Pattern recognition

Parameters of Cognitive Functioning
• Level of consciousness/alertness
• Orientation
• Attention & Concentration
• Memory – registration (immediate, recent, remote)
• Intelligence estimation
• Knowledge base/fund of information
• Capacity to read and write
• Abstraction/concrete thinking

Regional Brain Dysfunction

Frontal Lobe
- Impaired complex motor behavior
- Inability to repeat phrases with prosody
- Broca's aphasia (non-fluent)
- Impaired rapid sequential movements
- Impaired problem solving, judgment, concentration, and orientation

Temporal Lobe

Unilateral Dominant
- Memory problems
- Wernicke's aphasia (fluent)

Unilateral Non-dominant
- Impaired recognition of sounds
- Disorder of speech prosody

Bilateral
- Korsakoff's syndrome
- Klüver-Bucy syndrome+
- Language, memory, and emotion are affected
  - Writing and naming (neologisms are made-up words)
  - Gnosis – recognition of numbers and letters
  - Comprehension of spoken language

+ hypersexuality, hyperorality, psychic blindness, placidity

Parietal Lobe

Dominant
- Gerstmann's syndrome*
- Alexia with agraphia
- Astereognosis
- Language recognition and word memory impairment

Non-Dominant
- Disorders of spatial awareness (e.g. east-west orientation)
- Calculation problems

* agraphia, acalculia, finger agnosia and left-right disorientation

Occipital Lobe
- Anton's syndrome – cortical blindness and denial of blindness
- Balint's syndrome – gaze paralysis & abnormal guidance of limbs
- Agnosia for faces and colors
- Alexia (inability to read)

7. Major Clinical Disorders

Schizophrenia/Schizophreniform Dis.

Schizophrenia is characterized by:
• At least 1 month of **positive symptoms** (hallucinations, delusions, disorganized speech, and severe behavioral changes)
• A 6-month period of continuous disturbance involving **deficit** or **negative symptoms** (see p. 44 – 45) and which may include positive symptoms in either full-scale or attenuated form

Biological Features
• Genetic Risk – MZ twins 40%; both parents 25%; one parent 15%; DZ twins/one sibling 10%; general risk 1%
• Structural brain changes and neurochemical, neurophysiological, and endocrine abnormalities have been found on a consistent basis

Psychosocial Features
• There is currently no evidence to implicate psychosocial causes in the etiology of schizophrenia
• Family/interpersonal factors have a significant impact on the course of the illness: **schisms** (family divisions), **skews** (power imbalances), **double bind** (no-win situations), and **expressed emotion (EE)**, defined as being *critical*, *hostile*, or *overinvolved* with patients

Biological Treatment
• First episode psychosis should be investigated and managed on an inpatient basis; it is crucial to rule out substance use and general medical conditions that can cause psychosis
• Antipsychotic medication is the cornerstone of treatment
• Traditional antipsychotic medications work well for positive symptoms but are less effective for negative symptoms

Psychosocial Treatment
• Community care involves a case manager, vocational rehabilitation, social skills training, and ongoing supportive therapy
• Family education is important to lower the amount of EE
• Housing in a group home or residence may need to be arranged

Prognosis
• Overall, the prognosis remains discouraging: only 25% lead relatively normal lives; over 50% require repeated hospitalizations

Schizophrenia/Schizophreniform Dis.

"HALDOL BENDER"

Hallucinations – the most common type are auditory

Areas of function are impaired (social, occupational, etc.)

Length of the disturbance is 6 months or longer

Disorganized speech

Organic (general medical) causes have been excluded

Loosening of associations – a disorder of thought form

Behavioral changes – disorganized or catatonic behaviors

Exclude – Mood disorders (with psychotic features), schizoaffective disorder

Negative symptoms (see p. 44 – 45)

Delusions – usually bizarre in content (cannot possibly occur)

Early (pervasive developmental) disorders not present

Recreational drug use excluded – e.g. amphetamines & cocaine

Practice Points

• Schizophreniform Disorder shares most of the criteria with schizophrenia except:
• the duration is at least 1 month but less than 6 months
• the level of functioning is not necessarily disrupted to the same degree
• Positive symptoms respond better to antipsychotics than negative symptoms (which often predominate with time)
• Paranoid Schizophrenia tends to have a later onset and milder course than other forms; paranoid, schizotypal, and schizoid personality disorders are in the **schizophrenic spectrum** (p. 51)
• Good prognostic indicators are:
• family history of mood disorders; older age of onset
• psychotic symptoms starting soon after psychosocial decline
• confusion or perplexity when psychotic
• good level of adjustment prior to the onset of symptoms
• compliance with all types of treatment
• avoidance of recreational drug use
• no suicidal ideation or attempts at self-harm
• female gender

Positive & Negative Symptoms

Many clinicians divide the signs and symptoms of schizophrenia into positive and negative symptoms, also referred to as Type I and Type II, respectively. One way to conceptualize this distinction is that positive symptoms are *added* to the picture (that is they are not present in unaffected people). Positive symptoms are: **hallucinations**, **delusions**, **formal thought disorders**, and **bizarre** or **disorganized behavior**. Negative symptoms are *deficits* in the clinical presentation, and are normal/adaptive features that are present in people who do not suffer from schizophrenia. Part of developing skills as an interviewer is to not only pay attention to what *is* being said or done, but also to what *is not* being said or done. In many ways, negative symptoms contribute more to the disability suffered in schizophrenia than do the positive symptoms. Negative symptoms have a slow, insidious onset but impact on the patient's ability to work, live independently, and stay in relationships.

"NEGATIVE TRACK"

Negligible response to conventional antipsychotics

Eye contact is decreased

Grooming & hygiene decline

Affective responses become flat

Thought blocking

Inattentiveness

Volition is diminished

Expressive gestures decrease

Time – increases the number of negative symptoms

Recreational interests diminish; **R**elationships decrease

A's – absence/lack of certain features (see below for 5 A's)

Content of speech diminishes (poverty of thought)

Knowledge – cognitive deficits increase

a**P**athy/avolition
a**L**ogia
Affective flattening
a**N**hedonia
a**T**tentional impairment

PLANT mnemonic for the five A's from the Scale for the Assessment of Negative Symptoms (SANS) provided by: **Dr. David Wagner Indiana University**

Positive & Negative Symptoms

The distinction between negative and positive symptoms is important for several reasons:

• When Kraepelin and Bleuler first described schizophrenia, they made distinctions between fundamental (positive) and accessory (negative) symptoms. Bleuler suggested the term schizophrenia in 1911 to refer to a splitting or schism between thoughts, emotions, and behavior. Prior to this, Kraepelin referred to this illness as *dementia praecox* (literally, a premature dementia).

• Negative symptoms are not usually treated effectively by traditional antipsychotic medication, whereas positive symptoms generally respond more favorably. Newer (atypical) antipsychotics (e.g. clozapine, olanzapine, quetiapine, risperidone) appear to treat negative symptoms much more effectively.

• One of the five principal criteria for diagnosing schizophrenia is the presence of negative symptoms. The DSM-IV requires that a six-month period of illness be present to diagnose schizophrenia. This period can consist of active (positive) symptoms that are preceded by **prodromal symptoms** or followed by **residual symptoms**. Prodromal and residual symptoms may consist largely, or even exclusively, of negative symptoms.

• Negative symptoms become more prominent with time and are significantly disabling to patients. Statistically, those with primarily negative symptoms are unmarried males with an earlier onset, poorer course, and higher incidence of other behavioral abnormalities.

Dr. Nancy Andreason developed standardized scales to more fully assess the presence of positive and negative symptoms. The scale for positive symptoms is called the **SAPS (Scale for the Assessment of Positive Symptoms)**.

The other is the **SANS (Scale for the Assessment of Negative Symptoms)**. For those who appreciate puns, *sans* in French means "without." The major headings in the SANS scale are in the PLANT mnemonic on the previous page. The scales are available in major reference texts.

Hallucinations

Hallucinations are perceptions that occur when there is no actual stimulus present. They are the most severe of the disorders of perception. Additional features of hallucinations are that they:
• Occur in all sensory modalities
• Can be simple or complex
• Seem as vivid as real life experiences
• Occur spontaneously
• Are often intrusive
• Are internal experiences attributed to external sources

Hallucinations are given the following terms according to the sensory modalities in which they occur:

Sense	Name of Hallucination
sight	visual
sound	auditory
smell	olfactory
taste	gustatory
touch	somatic or tactile

Brief, poorly formed experiences are called **incomplete**, **unformed**, or **elementary hallucinations**. Examples are flashes of light, whispered sounds, faint odors or tastes, or the sensation of being gently nudged. **Hypnagogic hallucinations** occur while falling asleep, and **hypnopompic hallucinations** occur while awakening. These experiences occur in a large percentage of the population and are not considered to be pathological by themselves.

Auditory hallucinations are the most common type in psychiatric conditions. In general, they occur as distinctly heard voices that speak clearly formed words, or even have conversations. Some patients are instructed by a voice to perform an act; this experience is called a **command hallucination**. In medical (organic) conditions causing hallucinations, patients most often hear indistinct sounds such as ringing, grating, or humming. Visual hallucinations are the next most prevalent type encountered in psychiatric illnesses. It is more common to have visual and auditory hallucinations occurring together than it is to have visual hallucinations alone. Olfactory, gustatory, and somatic hallucinations usually have medical causes.

Delusions

A **delusion** is defined as a fixed, false belief that:
• Is inconsistent with cultural or subcultural norms
• Is inappropriate for the person's level of education
• Is not altered with proof to the contrary
• Preoccupies the thoughts of the patient
• Is not resisted by the patient
• Ranges from implausible to impossible

The content of delusions ranges from fragmented to systematized, and from situations that are possible (**non-bizarre**) to those that are impossible (**bizarre**). In cases where a patient appears to have a discrete, plausible, but false belief (e.g. "someone reads my mail"), it may only be possible to establish the presence of a delusion when collateral information becomes available. Cultural differences can also account for unusual ideas. In order to distinguish a delusion from other aberrations of thought content, it is crucial to establish that it is indeed fixed. For example, someone who is **confabulating** (making up historical information, but not being deliberately misleading) will change historical details when asked to repeat them.

Delusions that start *de novo* are called **primary delusions**. **Secondary delusions** arise out of a mood state, perceptual abnormality (including sensory deprivation or impairment), social factors, or other pre-existing psychopathology. Delusional patients demonstrate altered reasoning processes. **Apophony** (from the Greek "to become manifest") is the phenomenon in which arbitrary or false ideas are considered fact without adequate proof. This is also called **delusional intuition**. Events and objects become imbued with a personal, autistic significance.

Delusional patients make sweeping inferences based on small amounts of information (the process of **generalization**). They do not use their knowledge or experience to modify their beliefs. For example, a patient who passes through a radar trap (without speeding) would become convinced that "surveillance" was arranged so the police could monitor his or her actions. Delusions become a psychological compromise, and help to make sense of the internal chaos with which patients must contend (a process called **consolidation**).

Catatonia

Catatonia is a term applied to a diverse number of postural and movement disturbances. The motor disorders can include both increased and decreased levels of activity. The term catatonia was developed by Kahlbaum and initially was a diagnostic entity on its own. If Kahlbaum had been a dog person, he would have called it *dogatonia*.

In the DSM-IV, catatonia is diagnosable in three forms:
• As a subtype of schizophrenia
• As a specifier for a mood episode
• Due to a general medical condition

Catatonia is also found in:
• **Periodic catatonia** – a rare condition involving an alteration of thyroid function and nitrogen balance
• Neurologic illnesses that involve the basal ganglia, frontal lobes, limbic system, and extrapyramidal pathways
• Syphilis and viral encephalopathies
• Head trauma, arteriovenous malformations, etc.
• Toxic states (e.g. alcoholism, fluoride toxicity)
• Metabolic conditions (e.g. hypoglycemia, hyperparathyroidism)

This mnemonic incorporating the DSM-IV criteria for catatonia is:

"WRENCHES"

Weird (peculiar) movements
Rigidity
Echopraxia – copying the body movements of others
Negativism – automatic opposition to all requests
Catalepsy (waxy flexibility)
High level of motor activity
Echolalia – repeating the words of others
Stupor – immobility

Each of the letters in "WRENCHES" is explained in greater detail on the next page.

• Weird (peculiar) voluntary movements given as examples in the DSM-IV include: **inappropriate** or **bizarre postures**, **stereotyped movements**, **mannerisms**, and **grimacing**.

• **Rigidity**, which can present in the following ways:
  Lead pipe: resistance to movement in all directions
  Cogwheel: a stop-and-go pattern, as seen in Parkinsonism
  Clasp knife: resistance to a certain point, then giving way
Extreme rigidity can lead to muscle breakdown, acute renal failure, and in some cases, death (known as **lethal catatonia**).

• **Echopraxia** is the involuntary repetition of the movements of others (mimicry would be voluntary).

• **Negativism** refers to the automatic refusal to cooperate. Simple requests are strongly opposed for no obvious reason, even in cases where patients would benefit from participation (e.g. taking off a warm coat when inside). Patients typically either refuse, or do the exact opposite, of what is asked of them.

• **Catalepsy** (**waxy flexibility, flexibilitas cerea**) is a phenomenon whereby patients can be moved into new postures or positions and will stay this way for periods of thirty seconds or more.

• High level of motor activity, also called **catatonic excitement**, is an episode of hyperactive behavior consisting of a high-energy "running amok" that ends when the patient collapses in exhaustion or when treatment is initiated.

• **Echolalia** is the involuntary repetition of words, such as greetings, statements, and questions, without patients being able to express their own thoughts. Again, this differs from mimicry in that patients don't do this of their own volition.

• **Stupor** is probably the most commonly known catatonic behavior. Patients can show a decrease in movement to the point of being mute and akinetic; they may also have a reduced awareness of their environment. A stupor can last for a prolonged time, and even lead to the point where an intervention is necessary for nutritional or hygienic reasons. An episode can end abruptly with a sudden outburst or impulsive act that is not in response to external stimuli.

Speech Abnormalities

Abnormalities in speech reflect changes in the flow or process of thought. The ways in which speech can be affected in schizophrenia are numerous, and include the following:

Disturbance	Nature of Disturbance
Circumstantiality Tangentiality	• linkage between ideas is tight • sentence structure is maintained • overinclusive of detail (circumstantiality), or does not address the point (tangentiality)
Loose Associations	• words and sentences maintained • sentences are still properly constructed • connection between ideas is unclear, not obvious, or is nonsensical
Thought Blocking Thought Derailment	• syntax intact, but speech suddenly shifts (derailment) or halts (blocking) • patients may or may not return to the previous topic, and are unaware of what has happened
Fragmentation	• words intact but phrases become disconnected from each other
Verbigeration	• repetition of words and phrases (called **echolalia** if repeating another's words)
Jargon	• syntax intact but speech is meaningless
Word Salad	• words remain intact but all syntax is lost
Incoherence	• words are unintelligible

Neologisms are words made up by patients that have idiosyncratic meanings for them. Neologisms may be formed by the improper use of word sounds or other perceptual abnormalities. In psychiatric disorders, neologisms occur in syntactically correct places, as if they are words the interviewer should be familiar with.

The Schizophrenic Spectrum

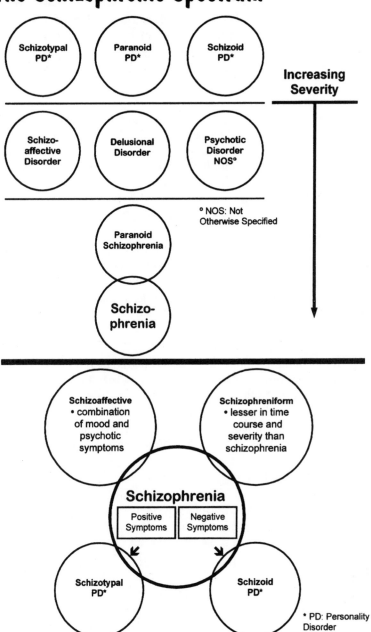

Delusional Disorder

Delusional Disorder (DD) is classified as a psychotic disorder. The delusions in DD are **non-bizarre** in nature, meaning the idea expressed is *possible*, even if it is not *probable*. In contrast, most of the delusions described by patients with schizophrenia are bizarre.

Biological Features

• Disease processes affecting the basal ganglia and limbic system can produce complex delusions
• Physical impairment and disabilities, especially with sensory deficits, can induce persecutory thoughts (e.g. poor vision or hearing)

Psychosocial Features

• DD is a rare disorder, with a reported prevalence of 0.03% (schizophrenia is about 30 times more common)
• Patients with DD often have very low self-esteem, fostered by an isolated environment, sadistic treatment, or unreliable caretakers
• Delusional disorder was previously called "paranoid disorder" – the name was changed to include other delusions (see p. 53) where persecution is not the central theme

Biological Treatment

• Delusional patients often resist taking medication
• Positive symptoms are often successfully treated with antipsychotics, but delusions typically have a poor response
• Some reports indicate pimozide may be useful for somatic delusions; serotonergic antidepressants have also been used
• If antipsychotics are effective, low doses are often sufficient

Psychosocial Treatment

• A wide range of psychotherapies can be used; therapy focuses on social integration instead of reducing delusional thinking
• Avoid either confronting, or colluding with, delusions
• Delusions often contain a "kernel" of truth

Prognosis

• The prognosis for DD is generally favorable; only about 25% of patients have no improvement in their symptoms
• 25% of patients are later re-diagnosed with another condition

Delusional Disorder
"NO FAME"
Non-bizarre delusions (e.g. improbable, not impossible)
One-month minimum duration

Functioning is not markedly impaired
Absence of other criteria for schizophrenia
Mood episodes are brief compared to the duration of illness
Exclusion of substance-related and general medical conditions

Types of Delusions
"J-PEGS"

> **J**ealous Type (Othello syndrome)
> **P**ersecutory Type
> **E**rotomanic Type (de Clérambault syndrome)
> **G**randiose Type
> **S**omatic Type

Practice Points
• Thoughts that are of less than delusional intensity are called **overvalued ideas**
• The main ego defense in paranoia is **projection** (attributing unacceptable inner experiences to others); other major defenses used are **denial** and **reaction formation**
• Kurt Schneider listed findings of particular value in diagnosing schizophrenia and called these **first-rank symptoms**. Of eleven first-rank symptoms, eight involve delusions that caused patients to feel under the control of external forces and to respond passively (also called delusions of passivity or passivity experiences).
• **Thought broadcasting** – patients experience their thoughts as being automatically broadcast to others (as if by television or radio)
• **Thought insertion** – thoughts are inserted from an outside source
• **Thought withdrawal** – thoughts are removed before being expressed
• **Insertion of somatic passivity** – submission to an external force
• **Insertion of feelings** – "made" or forced feelings
• **Insertion of impulses** – submission to an impulse
• **Insertion of an outside will** – passivity of volition
• **Delusional perception** – the attribution of false (delusional) meanings to ordinary events

Delusional Disorder

Delusions are given the suffix "mania" to denote an exaggerated interest in, or preference for something, but also implies a behavior or an action. Excessive ruminations are given the suffix "philia" indicating a disposition towards something. For example, *pyromania* refers to fire setting and *pyrophilia* refers to an excessive interest in fires. Despite their great variety, delusions fall into a set number of themes. As indicated below, delusions often relate to early developmental needs, struggles, and milestones. Common themes involve one's body, nonexistence, one's self, and the outside world. Common delusional themes can be related to **Erickson's Life Cycle Stages**:

Stage	Central Issue	Theme of Delusion
• Basic Trust vs. Basic Mistrust	Safety	Paranoia
• Autonomy vs. Shame & Doubt	Bodily Functions	Somatization
• Initiative vs. Guilt	Achievement	Grandiosity
• Industry vs. Inferiority	Achievement	Grandiosity
• Identity vs. Role Diffusion	Love	Jealousy & Erotomania
• Intimacy vs. Isolation	Love	Jealousy & Erotomania

Culture-Bound Syndromes

A sampling of syndromes from other cultures . . .
• **Brain Fag** – belief that the brain can suffer fatigue from overuse
• **Koro** – belief that the penis or vulva will recede into the body and cause death (differentiate this from **kuru** which is a slow virus infection causing neurologic degeneration)
• **Rootwork/mal puesto** – belief that one can subject others, or be subjected to, hexes, spells, or curses
• **Taijin kyofusho** – the belief that one's body or its parts and functions are offensive to others
• **Windigo** – delusion that one can be transformed into a giant monster that eats human flesh
• **Zar** – delusional possession by a spirit

Some Common Delusions

- **Animal metamorphosis** – cat (galeanthropy), dog (cynanthropy), wolf (lycanthropy)
- **Cacodaemonomania** – being poisoned by an evil spirit
- **Caesarmania** – delusion of grandiose ability (or inventing a garlic-laden salad)
- **Capgras' Syndrome** – an impostor has replaced someone significant to the patient and has an identical appearance; also called negative misidentification (e.g. "It looks like my wife, but I know that it is not her.")
- **Delusion of Reference** – ascribing personal meaning to common events; often involves the TV, newspapers, or radio having special messages just for the patient, but can include idiosyncratic associations (e.g. a bird flew by, therefore my car is low on oil)
- **Dorian Gray** – the person stays the same age while everyone else ages
- **Enosimania** – guilt or worthlessness for having committed some catastrophic deed
- **Folie à deux** – a delusion is transferred from a psychotic person to a recipient who accepts the belief
- **Folie induite** – transfer of a delusion to someone who is already psychotic; a delusion added to a pre-existing one
- **Fregoli's Syndrome** – a persecutor impersonates people the patient sees; also called positive misidentification (e.g. "These people look different, but I know they are all my enemy in disguise.")
- **Intermetamorphosis** – a familiar person (usually a persecutor) and a misidentified stranger share both physical and psychological attributes
- **Magical Thinking** – believing that an event will occur simply by wishing it so, as if by magic
- **Messianic** – being God (also called theomania)
- **Mignon** – being of royal lineage
- **Nihilism** – nonexistence; loss of organs, body or everything; damnation; sense of death or disintegration; also called Cotard's syndrome
- **Phantom Boarder** – unwelcome delusional house guests
- **Poverty** – loss of all wealth and property
- **Reduplicative Paramnesia** – thinking that people, places, or body parts have been duplicated (heutoscopy is also the delusion of having a double)

Schizoaffective Disorder

Schizoaffective Disorder is listed as an "other psychotic disorder" in the DSM-IV. As the name implies, both psychotic and mood symptoms are present. The DSM-IV changed "affective disorders" to "mood disorders," however, the name of this condition was not changed to schizomood disorder – maybe because it sounds funny. Diagnosing this condition involves three steps:

Part 1

Main Criteria for Schizophrenia
• delusions
• hallucinations
• disorganized speech
• behavioral changes
• negative symptoms

Two of the above are present at the same time as symptoms causing a mood disturbance (manic, depressed, or a mixed state)

Part 2

Psychotic Component

• delusions, or
• hallucinations are present for at least 2 weeks without prominent mood symptoms

Part 3

Mood Component

• depression, or
• mania, or a
• mixed episode is present for a substantial period of the total illness

Practice Points

• Considerable debate exists as to whether schizoaffective disorder is primarily a psychotic disorder, a mood disorder (bipolar type), a hybrid of both, or a distinct disorder
• Schizoaffective Disorder has a prognosis intermediate between schizophrenia and mood disorders; patients with the bipolar subtype tend to fare better than those with the depressive subtype
• In general, patients require continual treatment for their mood symptoms and intermittent treatment for psychotic symptoms
• The criteria were constructed to avoid diagnosing mood disorders with psychotic features as schizoaffective disorder

Brief Psychotic Disorder

Brief Psychotic Disorder is defined as having a duration of at least one day, and remitting in less than one month. During this period, at least one of the following psychotic symptoms must be present:
• Hallucinations
• Delusions
• Disorganized speech
• Behavioral abnormalities (gross disorganization or catatonia)

These are the same criteria for schizophrenia, minus the negative symptoms. Brief psychotic disorders are often precipitated by major life events. The presence of certain personality disorders also seems to predispose individuals to having brief psychotic disorders: borderline, histrionic, narcissistic, paranoid, and schizotypal. Up to 75% of patients have no recurrence. The following symptoms are more characteristic of a brief psychotic disorder than schizophrenia: significant emotional lability, screaming, confusion, poor memory, and extremes of behavior. This illness has also been called **reactive psychosis**, **psychogenic psychosis**, and **boufée déliriante**.

Time Line for Diagnosing Psychotic Disorders

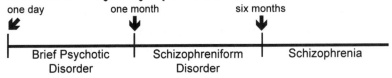

one day	one month	six months
Brief Psychotic Disorder	Schizophreniform Disorder	Schizophrenia

Shared Psychotic Disorder

Shared Psychotic Disorder is also known as *folie à deux*, or double insanity. It has also been called *folie imposée* (imposed insanity) and *folie simultanée* (simultaneous insanity). In this condition, one person (the primary case) suffers from a psychotic disorder, and imparts delusional beliefs to another. In most situations, the inducer is related to the inducee, and has a dominant role (parent, older sibling, etc.). Social isolation is also a factor that facilitates the transmission and acceptance of delusional beliefs. This disorder can extend beyond two people, and is called *folie à trois* when it involves three people, *folie à quatre* for four, etc.

Major Depressive Disorder/Episode

A Major Depressive Disorder (**MDD**) is one of two main mood disorders, the other being bipolar disorder. While a transient decline in mood is a universal human experience, depression is characterized by hopelessness, a sense of losing control, and a loss of enjoyment.

Biological Features
• Genetic factors are becoming increasingly evident; adoption and twin studies also support this finding (chromosomes 5, 11, 18, X)
• Serotonin and norepinephrine are the neurotransmitters involved in mood disorders; antidepressant medications increase their levels
• There are several biological changes in depression, e.g. sleep & circadian rhythm changes; endocrine & immune system changes

Psychosocial Features
• Lifetime prevalence for men is 15%; for women it is 25 to 30%
• Stressful events early in life may predispose to mood disorders
• Freud focused on the issue of loss in the etiology of depression
• Frequently there are stressors (actual or symbolic) that occur prior to the onset of depression

Biological Treatment
• Antidepressants from different chemical classes appear to have similar efficacy, but vary widely in their side effect profile
• Specific treatments may be indicated for subtypes of depression
• Onset of action takes at least 2 weeks and appears to be related to down-regulation of post-synaptic beta noradrenergic receptors and type-2 serotonergic ($5HT_2$) receptors

Psychosocial Treatment
• Many effective psychotherapies exist for depression: cognitive, interpersonal, and psychodynamic are the most common
• Combining psychotherapy with medication may produce the best outcome, though this issue is still debated

Prognosis
• The prognosis for MDE is generally favorable; at least 80% of patients fully recover; relapses are common with up to 25% occurring in the first year, 50% within 2 years, and 75% within 5 years

Major Depressive Disorder/Episode

"MASS FEE GAP FITS"

Mood is depressed for most of the day, almost everyday*
Activities are no longer of interest or pleasurable (anhedonia)*
Sleep changes – insomnia or hypersomnia*
Suicidal ideation*

Functioning is significantly impaired
Energy level is decreased*
Exclude – mixed episode and bereavement

Guilt or worthlessness that is excessive or inappropriate*
Appetite changes (up or down); weight changes by 5% or more*
Psychomotor changes – agitation or retardation*

Five of nine symptoms needed (marked with the asterisk *)
Indecisiveness, poor concentration, or diminished attention span*
Two-week minimum duration
Substance-Related Disorder needs to be excluded

Practice Points
• Electroconvulsive Therapy (**ECT**) is efficacious in depression with psychotic features in up to 80% of patients (and works faster than medication); neuroleptics with antidepressants are effective in about 60% of patients (see p. 197)
• Monoamine oxidase inhibitors (**MAOIs**) may be more effective in treating depressive episodes that have atypical features or prominent anxiety symptoms
• Buproprion is an antidepressant that appears to work by increasing dopamine levels
• Beta-blockers, benzodiazepines, and corticosteroids are the most common iatrogenic causes of depression
• Common augmentation strategies include: adding lithium, T_3, stimulants, or neuroleptics to an antidepressant; using antidepressants in combination is another strategy

Major Depressive Disorder/Episode

"SAD IMAGES" *

Sleep changes – insomnia or hypersomnia
Appetite changes (up or down); weight changes by 5% or more
Depressed mood for most of the day, almost everyday

Indecisiveness, poor concentration, and/or diminished attention span
Movements altered – psychomotor agitation or retardation
Activities are no longer of interest or pleasurable (anhedonia)
Guilt or worthlessness that is excessive or inappropriate
Energy level is decreased (fatigue)
Suicidal ideation

Practice Points

* The above mnemonic contains the nine DSM-IV criteria
• **Anomie** is a (real or imagined) lack of integration into society, leaving few social supports for the person
• **Apathy** is a "lack of feeling" characterized by diminished energy and interest in the environment; such patients are unemotional and listless; apathy has been described as a mood state and occurs with frontal lobe damage, schizophrenia, depression, and substance abuse (e.g. sedatives, marijuana, etc.)
• **Alexithymia** is the inability to sense and describe mood states; patients are "disconnected" from their feelings and describe them in terms of physical sensations or behaviors; this is seen in schizophrenia, posttraumatic stress disorder, and somatoform disorders
• **Euthymia** is the word used to describe normal mood
• The criteria used to diagnose the dysphoric mood states of depression, cyclothymia, and dysthymia are different (see p. 64)
• There is no clear method for distinguishing sustained affect from reactive mood. Certain conditions (e.g. personality disorders, substance abuse) in which there is a good deal of variation in the moment-to-moment expression of emotion can occur comorbidly with mood disorders. To complicate matters, there is a variant of a bipolar mood disorder called a **mixed state**, where manic and depressive symptoms occur simultaneously.

Melancholic Features Specifier
"PAGER MAD"

Psychomotor changes are marked (retardation or agitation)

Anorexia or weight loss

Guilt is excessive or inappropriate

Early morning awakening

Reactivity is lacking to stimuli that are usually pleasurable

Morning depression is regularly worse

Anhedonia (activities bring no pleasure)

Distinct quality of depressed mood

Practice Points

• Melancholic features are thought to indicate a type of depression that is likely to respond to medication

• A mood disturbance with these features has been referred to as endogenous (lacking an obvious precipitant), as opposed to a depression with obvious precipitants (called a **reactive depression**)

Atypical Features Specifier
"RAILS"

Reactivity of mood – changes with positive experiences

Appetite increases – hyperphagia

Interpersonal rejection sensitivity

Leaden paralysis – limbs feels as if they are made of lead

Sleep is increased – hypersomnia

Practice Points

• The presence of atypical features may indicate a form of depression that may be preferentially responsive to MAOIs or SSRIs

• Atypical features may also indicate that the depressive episode is part of a bipolar mood disorder, and that the patient may in time develop manic or hypomanic episodes

Bipolar Mood Disorder

Bipolar Disorder/Bipolar Mood Disorder (**BMD**) refers to the presence of manic episodes and major depressive episodes, and is also called **manic-depressive illness**. Even if patients suffer only manic episodes, this is still the diagnosis given. BMD usually starts with an episode of depression, and has an average age of onset 10 years earlier (about 30 years) than MDD (about 40 years).

Biological Features
• Genetic correlates are stronger for BMD than for MDD; over 90% of patients have a relative with a mood disorder
• **Kindling** is the repeated sub-threshold stimulation of a nerve cell that eventually causes it to fire; temporal lobe kindling may be a factor in the etiology of the mood changes seen in BMD
• Neuro-imaging has revealed ventricular enlargement more consistently in BMD than in depression

Psychosocial Features
• BMD has a lifetime prevalence of 1% with an equal sex ratio
• BMD occurs more frequently in higher socio-economic classes

Biological Treatment
• Mood stabilizers (lithium, carbamazepine, valproate) are the mainstay of treatment for BMD
• Management of an acute manic episode requires a neuroleptic or benzodiazepine (i.e. clonazepam); second-line medication for BMD includes clozapine, verapamil, and clonidine (among others)

Psychosocial Treatment
• During depressive phases psychotherapy can be helpful
• Education for patients and families is crucial; principal teaching points involve the course of the illness, the benefits of compliance, and warning signs of an impending manic or depressive episode

Prognosis
• The prognosis for BMD is less favorable than for MDD
  • 50% of patients have another manic episode within 2 years
  • only 10% of patients are free from future manic episodes
  • 30% of bipolar patients have chronic symptoms that impair their ability to function in social, occupational, and academic roles

Manic/Hypomanic Episode
"FAST DIGGERS"

Functioning is severely impaired

Activities pursued with the potential for painful consequences*

Substance-Related Disorders need to be excluded

Talkative – both *rate* and *amount* of speech are increased*

Distractibility*

Ideas racing (flight of ideas)*

Grandiose; inflated self-esteem*

Goal-directed activity is increased*

Elevated or **E**xpansive mood (can also be irritable)

Rule out general medical conditions

Sleep requirement is lessened*

Practice Points

* With irritable mood, 4/7 criteria are required; with an elevated or expansive mood, 3/7 are required to make this diagnosis (the DSM-IV criteria are marked with an *)

• A hypomanic episode differs from mania as follows:
  • symptoms only need to be present for 4 days (vs. 7 for mania)
• the ability to function in important roles is not impaired
• hospitalization is not required, and there are no psychotic symptoms

• A course specifier for BMD is called *Rapid Cycling*:
  • this involves 4 or more episodes of mood disturbance within 1 year
  • a cycle is the recovery (full or partial) from the most current mood disturbance (i.e. euthymic mood for at least two months), or a switch to the opposite mood polarity
  • cycling can be triggered by antidepressants and thyroid dysfunction
  • this subtype has a poor response to lithium

• *Seasonal Pattern* and *Postpartum Onset* are course specifiers

• Ask about manic/hypomanic symptoms in all depressed patients

• Manic episodes can be caused by: multiple sclerosis, head injuries, Huntington's disease, epilepsy, and corticosteroid use

• Elevated mood states occur in schizophrenia (disorganized type), substance abuse (usually with stimulants), dementia, and delirium

Dysthymic Disorder

"HE TAILS"

Hopelessness
Esteem is decreased

Two-year duration (minimum)
Appetite changes (up or down)
Indecisiveness
Lethargy, **L**ow energy
Sleep changes (increased or decreased)

Dysthymic Disorder (DD) (dysthymic means "ill humored") is a chronic mood disturbance. DD lacks the severity and episodic nature of a major depressive disorder. This diagnosis is common (3% prevalence) and can be a feature of other disorders, sharing a particular overlap with the borderline personality disorder. One-third of patients develop a more serious mood disorder. Antidepressants and cognitive therapy are effective treatment modalities.

Cyclothymic Disorder

Cyclothymic Disorder (CD) is characterized by the presence of mood fluctuations that do not reach manic highs or major depressive lows. At one point it was considered a personality disorder. The current concept of CD overlaps with the borderline personality disorder and other Cluster B personalities. CD is a chronic disorder that must be present over at least two years. Mood fluctuation can occur over the course of hours. Episodes with mixed symptoms are also common. One-third of patients eventually develop a more serious mood disorder, often a **Bipolar II Disorder** (hypomania and depression; a **Bipolar I Disorder** is mania and depression; **Bipolar III Disorder** is antidepressant-induced mania/hypomania). Mood stabilizers are indicated in the same doses as for bipolar disorders. However, antidepressants should be used cautiously because they can precipitate manic or hypomanic episodes (particularly tricyclics – newer antidepressants seem less likely to do this).

Mood Disorder Patterns

Manic
Hypomanic
Euthymic
Depressive Symptoms
Major Depression

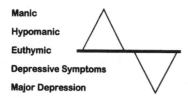

Bipolar Disorder Type I

• Manic and Depressive Episodes
• Depressive Episodes in some patients are brief or nonexistent
• No separate diagnostic category exists for Unipolar Mania

Manic
Hypomanic
Euthymic
Depressive Symptoms
Major Depression

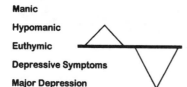

Bipolar Disorder Type II

• Hypomania with Major Depressive Episodes; the implications of the distinction from Bipolar Type I are still being investigated

Manic
Hypomanic
Euthymic
Depressive Sx.
Major Depression

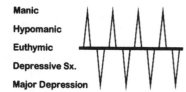

Rapid Cycling Type

• 4 or more episodes of Mania, Hypomania, Mixed, or MDE in 1 year
• Recovery for 2 months between episodes, or a switch to a mood episode of opposite polarity

Manic
Hypomanic
Euthymic
Depressive Sx.
Major Depression

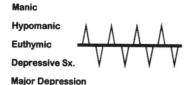

Cyclothymic Disorder

• Depressive symptoms do not necessarily meet the criteria for a Dysthymic Disorder and are not as severe as an MDE; highs can be hypomanic in intensity

Manic
Hypomanic
Euthymic
Depressive Sx.
Major Depression

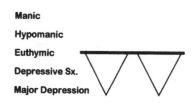

Major Depressive Episode

• Depressive symptoms are of significant duration & severity; usual course is a full recovery, but may have future episodes (the example here shows **recurrent episodes**)

Manic
Hypomanic
Euthymic
Depressive Sx.
Major Depression

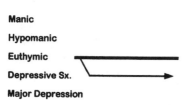

Dysthymic Disorder

• Depressive symptoms are not severe enough for an MDE
• Some patients do develop a coexisting MDE; this is then called a **Double Depression**

Mood Disorders – Describing Mood

Mood is evaluated according to the following parameters:
- Quality
- Reactivity
- Intensity
- Stability

Quality

Quality of mood is the patient's reported emotional state. The DSM-IV includes the following mood types:
- Depressed
- Euphoric
- Anxious
- Angry/Irritable

Reactivity

Reactivity is the degree to which mood is altered by external factors. Mood can be shifted by events, the environment, or interactions with others. Manic patients often escalate in mood with stimulation. Depressed patients may feel worse in the morning and have their spirits lift as the day progresses. Similarly, anxious or angry patients have a waxing and waning of their mood under certain conditions.

Intensity

Intensity refers to the degree to which the mood is expressed. Like affect, mood has depth, amount, or amplitude. Two patients can experience depressed mood with a similarly flat affect and restricted range of emotional expression. One patient may appear lethargic, withdrawn, and show little interest in the interview. The other patient may have problems with concentration, lowered self-esteem, and be able to convey the degree to which this episode has interfered with his or her life. The difference between these patients is the depth or intensity of their mood states.

Stability

Stability or duration describes the length of time the mood disturbance exists without significant variation. Mood disorders are required to have a specific time course:

MDD – 2 weeks   *Manic Episode* – 1 week
Dysthymia – 2 years   *Cyclothymia* – 2 years

Mood Disorders – Mood vs. Affect

Mood is a person's internal feeling state. It is described by the patient (subjective), and refers to the pervasive emotional tone displayed throughout the interview. Mood is considered the "background" whereas affect is the "foreground." Affect refers to the visible, objective manifestations of an emotional state. It records momentary changes in the expression of emotional responses. Both internal (e.g. memories) and external events (e.g. aspects of the environment) can change affect. Affect can be likened to one's degree of satisfaction with the courses of a meal, while mood is the enjoyment of the entire evening. Affect is evaluated according to:

Type/Quality
There are nine principal types of affect:
- fear/anxiety
- interest
- surprise
- disgust
- shame
- contentment
- happiness
- anger
- sadness

Range
A *narrow* or *restricted* range of affect describes patients who express one or two emotional states. A *wide* or *expanded* range describes situations where several emotions are expressed.

Degree
Degree is the extent or intensity to which emotions are expressed.

Stability
Stability refers to the duration of an affective response.

Reactivity
Reactivity of affect refers to the degree to which external factors influence emotional expression.

Appropriateness
Appropriateness is the degree to which visible emotions match thought content.

Congruence
The association between affect and:
- Mood
- Appearance
- Behavior

Mood Disorders – Flight of Ideas

Flight of ideas is non-goal directed speech that "takes off" from the topic at hand. Patients are usually distractible, and change the topic every sentence or two. Speech remains logical, and the connections between ideas are still recognizable. Patients don't elaborate on their ideas before moving onto another topic. Their statements contain proper words and grammar. Flight of ideas differs from **tangential speech** in that topic changes are more abrupt, more frequent, and often prompted by a word in a previous sentence. Patients with flight of ideas speak in a pressured manner. In order to visualize flight of ideas, the following representation will be used:

A•B•C•D•E•F•G•H•I•J•K•L•M•N•O•P•Q•R•S•T•U•V•W•X•Y•Z

where:
• Each letter represents a word
• The alphabetical sequence indicates proper syntax
• Progression from left to right indicates a logical sequence
• The letters in flight of ideas are shown with brackets to indicate that the connections may or may not be obvious to the interviewer

Flight of Ideas

A•(B)(C)(D)(E)(F)(G)(H)(I)(J)(K)(L)(M)

Question Posed

A•B•C•D•E•F•G•H•I•J•K•L•M•

Direct Answer

Question Posed: *"Name the Seven Dwarfs."*
Direct Answer: *Dopey, Doc, Bashful, Happy, Grumpy, Sneezy, Sleepy*
Flight of Ideas: *"Happily, I don't think on such a small level. Small things come in good packages. I cut myself opening my mail yesterday, it still stings. I got stung by a bee last summer, but it's only fair, since I eat honey. I have breakfast every morning because it is the most important meal of the day. I like to eat three squares when I can, but not out of the can. Cans keep food around for years, but not if you take the label off. I bought a labeling machine, and now everything in my house has a proper name.*

Mood Disorders – Practice Points

Practice Points

• The terms **mood-congruent** and **mood-incongruent** are applied to delusions and hallucinations (psychotic features) that occur with mood disorders.

• The themes of depression are: guilt, worthlessness, death, failure, hopelessness, punishment, illness, etc. If the content of delusions in depressed patients forms along these lines, the term mood-congruent is applied.

• In manic episodes, mood-congruent delusions follow the themes of: power, brilliance, wealth, longevity, achievement, special relationships or connections, knowledge, etc.

• Manic patients with delusions of nihilism, poverty, or inadequacy have mood-incongruent delusions, as do depressed patients with delusions of grandeur, omnipotence, or relationships to famous people. Mood-incongruent delusions are a poor prognostic sign and may indicate the presence of a psychotic disorder.

• Depressed mood is often accompanied by changes in:
  • appearance (decline in self-care)
  • behavior (few spontaneous movements)
  • speech (speak softly, have little to say, etc.)
  • affect (restricted range, variable intensity)
  • thought content (morbid themes)
  • thought form (increased latency of responses)
  • diminished cognitive functioning

• Euphoric mood often occurs with changes in:
  • appearance (unusual or bizarre changes)
  • behavior (rapid, continual movements)
  • speech (speak loudly, have a great deal to say, etc.)
  • affect (expanded range, labile, intense)
  • thought content (grandiose themes)
  • thought form (flight of ideas, pressure of speech)
  • cognitive functions may be enhanced (creativity or word associations) or diminished because of distractibility

• A large number of '**d**' words describe feelings of depression: down, dejected, despondent, demoralized, dysphoric, despairing, dour, dispirited, drained, doleful, downcast, down in the dumps, desperate, defeated, dreary, disappointed, disillusioned, dissatisfied, disaffected, disconsolate, and downhearted.

• There are a large number of '**e**' words that describe feelings of mania: energized, elevated, elated, entertaining, exalted, extreme, expansive, extraordinary, ecstatic, effervescent, excited, effusive, and ebullient.

Panic Attack/Panic Disorder

A panic attack is a discrete episode of intense discomfort involving neurologic, cardiovascular, gastrointestinal, and psychic symptoms. Panic disorder consists of recurrent, unexpected panic attacks which are followed by one month of: continual concern about future attacks; worry about the consequences of an attack; and significantly altered behavior. Panic attacks aren't a distinct disorder in DSM-IV.

Biological Features
• Several substances can induce panic attacks: caffeine, inhalation of CO_2, infusion of lactate, and yohimbine (an alpha$_2$ antagonist)
• Central noradrenergic and peripheral autonomic hyperactivity account for many of the somatic features of panic disorder
• Panic disorder appears to have a distinct genetic component

Psychosocial Features
• The lifetime prevalence of panic attacks is 5%, and 2% for panic disorder; women appear twice as likely to be affected
• Panic attacks can be considered an adult form of **separation anxiety**; patients may have a history of this condition
• This disorder involves an exaggerated response to conditions that are misinterpreted as threatening (e.g. bodily sensations)
• Psychosocial stressors commonly precipitate panic attacks

Biological Treatment
• TCAs, MAOIs, SSRIs, and benzodiazepines can all be effective
• Beta-blockers and buspirone are ineffective for this condition
• Panic attacks can be treated acutely with benzodiazepines

Psychosocial Treatment
• Cognitive-behavioral therapies can be at least as efficacious as somatic treatments; combining both may be the most effective
• In vivo exposure and relaxation training are also used

Prognosis
• This has a favorable outcome – 80% of patients are either symptom free or affected only mildly over the span of years; agoraphobia, mood disorders, or substance-related disorders worsen the prognosis – up to 50% of patients develop one of these conditions

Panic Attack/Panic Disorder

"THIS ISN'T FUN"

Trembling
Hot flashes
Increased heart rate
Sweating

Inspiration – intake of air feels obstructed, choking sensation
Smothering, **S**hortness of breath
Numbness or tingling in the limbs (paresthesias)
Tightness in the chest

Fear of: losing control, going crazy, or dying
Unreal sense of: self (**depersonalization**)
        the environment (**derealization**)
Nausea or abdominal distress

Practice Points
• **Anticipatory anxiety** is the apprehensive expectation of another panic attack; this can become so pervasive that it is difficult to distinguish from generalized anxiety disorder
• Hyperthyroidism, pheochromocytoma, and hypoglycemia are common medical causes for panic attacks
• Typical situations that induce panic attacks are: driving a motor vehicle, crossing a bridge, and leaving one's neighborhood or city
• States of anxiety decrease blood flow to the frontal regions of the brain; some asymmetry of cerebral blood flow has been found in patients who suffer from panic attacks
• The presence of mitral valve prolapse (MVP) is not a significant factor in the treatment or prognosis of this disorder
• It is unusual for the onset of this disorder to occur after age 45
• Vertigo, parathyroid dysfunction, carcinoid syndrome, and porphyria are rarer medical causes of panic attacks

Phobic Disorders

A phobia is characterized by:
• A marked and persistent fear of an object or situation
• Immediate anxiety upon exposure to the object/situation
• Avoidance of the object or situation

The DSM-IV lists two major categories of phobic disorders:
• Social Phobia (social anxiety disorder)
• Specific Phobia (subtypes are Animal, Natural Environment, Blood-Injection-Injury, Situational, and Other – see p. 74)

Biological Features
• Behavioral inhibition is a temperamental factor
• Patients with phobias may have strong vasovagal responses
• Family studies provide some evidence for genetic transmission

Psychosocial Features
• Phobias affect up to 10% of the population
• **Displacement** and **symbolization** are key ego defenses

Biological Treatment
• Specific Phobias do not have a recommended drug treatment
• Social Phobias respond more favorably to medication:
    • performance anxiety can be treated with propranolol
    • generalized social phobia is often responsive to phenelzine

Psychosocial Treatment
• Phobias can be treated with cognitive-behavioral approaches such as in vivo exposure, relaxation training, self-talk, and self-hypnosis
• Psychodynamic approaches treat social phobia as part of a larger character disturbance (e.g. avoidant personality disorder)
• Psychodynamic psychotherapy seeks to discover the unconscious issues creating the phobia

Prognosis
• The prognosis for phobic disorders is generally favorable:
    • 80% of patients with specific phobias improve
    • social phobia tends to be lifelong with a waxing and waning course
    • comorbid conditions (depression, other anxiety disorders and substance-related disorders) are common and worsen the prognosis

Phobic Disorders
"FEARED"

Fear that is excessive and unreasonable
Exposure to the stimulus provokes anxiety
Avoids the phobic situation or object
Recognizes that the fear is excessive
Exclusion of other mental disorders (e.g. OCD, PTSD)
Distress is experienced in the feared situation

Practice Points
• **Learning Theory** factors that are thought to be operative in the development of phobias are:
Classical Conditioning, which involves coupling a neutral stimulus with one that evokes a response, so that over time the neutral stimulus causes the same reaction (e.g. Pavlov's dogs salivating at the sound of a bell), and
Operant Conditioning, where learning occurs on a trial and error basis, with responses being reinforced with rewards or punishments
• Psychoanalytic theory proposes that unacceptable impulses (i.e. sexual or aggressive) arouse a conflict causing anxiety, which then leads to the recruitment of an ego defense:

Instinctual drive causing conflict
↓
Signal anxiety to the ego
↓
Use of repression as the primary defense
↓
Use of displacement or symbolization as secondary defenses
↓
Development of a phobia

• The phobic stimulus may have a connection with the source of the conflict (called **symbolization**), e.g. a fear of trains in a patient with **separation anxiety**
• Freud developed his theory of phobias through his work with Little Hans, a boy who displaced his Oedipal conflict from his father onto horses and developed a phobia of them (sort of a reverse *Equus*)
• **Counterphobic attitude** refers to the process whereby patients deny their phobic anxiety and seek feared objects or situations; this most commonly arises as a reaction to serious medical conditions

Phobic Disorders

"ASP & BOAS" *

Animal type – e.g. attack chihuahuas or goldfish
Situational type – e.g. bridges, tunnels, flying, driving, etc.
People (social phobia) – e.g. public speaking

Blood/Injection – e.g. seeing blood or getting a needle
Other – used when other categories simply won't do
Agoraphobia – avoidance of places where escape or
getting help is difficult
Surroundings – elements in the natural environment such
as storms, water, heights, etc.

* For those unfamiliar with reptilian suborder *ophidia*, an asp is a venomous snake (viper), and also makes an excellent Scrabble® word; this mnemonic is helpful because snakes are a common phobia (even for Indiana Jones).

• **Agoraphobia** is derived from Greek and means "fear of the marketplace." The DSM-IV defines it as *anxiety about being in places or situations from which escape might be difficult (or embarrassing) or in which help may not be available in the event of having an unexpected or situationally predisposed panic attack or panic-like symptoms*. Agoraphobia is a common phobia and the one that causes the greatest impairment of social and occupational functioning. Generally, patients who experience repeated panic attacks become "phobic" of the places where attacks occur, or where help or escape are difficult to arrange. Patients with agoraphobia curtail their activities significantly. They make constant demands on friends and family members to accompany them on outings. Agoraphobia is frequently complicated by other phobias or obsessions. Additionally, depressive disorders and substance abuse often complicate the lives of agoraphobics.

Agoraphobia is coded in the DSM-IV in the following:
• Panic Disorder with/without Agoraphobia
• Agoraphobia Without History of Panic Disorder

Specific Phobias

- Anginaphobia – fear of narrowness
- Anuptophobia – fear of staying single
- Cherophobia – fear of good news
- Dementophobia – fear of insanity
- Ergophobia – fear of work
- Gelophobia – fear of laughing
- Genuphobia – fear of knees
- Glossophobia – fear of talking
- Gymnophobia – fear of naked bodies
- Herpetophobia – fear of lizards
- Iatrophobia – fear of doctors
- Kainophobia – fear of newness
- Kenophobia – fear of empty spaces
- Kleptophobia – fear of stealing
- Logophobia – fear of words
- Methyphobia – fear of alcohol
- Mnemonophobia – fear of memories
- Musophobia – fear of mice
- Myxophobia – fear of slime
- Neopharmaphobia – fear of new drugs
- Osmophobia – fear of smells
- Panphobia – fear of everything
- Pentheraphobia – fear of mother-in-law
- Phobophobia – fear of fear itself
- Polyphobia – fear of many things
- Psychophobia – fear of the mind
- Sinistrophobia – fear of things "of the left" (e.g. left-handedness)
- Sitophobia – fear of food or eating
- Sophophobia – fear of learning
- Tridecaphobia – fear of the number 13

From: **The Encyclopedia of Phobias, Fears, and Anxieties**
R. Doctor, Ph.D. & A. Khan
Facts on File, Inc., New York, 1989

Obsessive-Compulsive Disorder

Obsessive-Compulsive Disorder (**OCD**) is characterized by:
• Obsessions – recurrent thoughts, impulses, or images
• Compulsions – conscious, repetitive behaviors or mental acts
OCD can be diagnosed by the presence of either obsessions or compulsions. Obsessions are recognized as products of the patient's own mind (as opposed to **thought insertion**). The intrusive nature of obsessions causes anxiety, which is lessened by the compulsion.

Biological Features
• Serotonin dysregulation is the leading biochemical hypothesis
• Intractable OCD is treated by lesioning the cingulum
• About 35% of patients have affected family members
• About 25% of OCD patients have tics, and 25% of patients with tics have OCD (both involve the basal ganglia)

Psychosocial Features
• The lifetime prevalence of OCD is about 2% (equal sex ratio)
• OCD differs from the obsessive-compulsive personality disorder; most OCD patients do not have this personality disorder premorbidly
• The major ego defenses used in OCD are: **isolation (of affect)**, **undoing**, **magical thinking**, and **intellectualization**
• Learning theory proposes that compulsions, like phobias, are conditioned stimuli

Biological Treatment
• Serotonin reuptake inhibitors are used; the treatment of choice is clomipramine and the SSRIs; the doses required are similar to those used to treat depressive disorders
• MAOIs, buspirone, neuroleptics, and fenfluramine are also used; augmentation with lithium has also been successful

Psychosocial Treatment
• **Exposure** and **response prevention** are the behavioral interventions most frequently used
• Psychodynamic approaches focus on the handling of impulses

Prognosis
• About 70% have at least moderate improvement in their symptoms

Obsessive-Compulsive Disorder

"A BIT FORCED"

Attempts are made to ignore or suppress obsessions

Behaviors are not realistically connected with the obsession
Interferes with normal routine (social or occupational functioning)
Time consuming – takes up more than 1 hour per day

Feels anxious – OCD is an anxiety disorder
Obsessions
Recognizes obsessions are a product of own mind
Compulsions
Excessive nature of obsessions and compulsions is appreciated
Distressing to the patient (ego-dystonic)

OCD symptoms generally follow certain patterns (listed in decreasing order of frequency):

Obsession	Corresponding Compulsion
• contamination	• cleaning (of self or articles)
• doubt (impending doom)	• checking (stoves, locks, etc.)
• intrusive derogatory, aggressive, or sexual thoughts	• usually occur without compulsions may involve mental acts
• symmetry, neatness, precision	• perfection, leading to obsessional slowness

• Compulsions are usually behaviors, but can also consist of mental acts such as repeating phrases or names
• Depressive symptoms and major depressive episodes are common in patients with OCD; non-suppression on the **dexamethasone suppression test** (**DST**) is seen in 30% of patients with OCD
• Other anxiety disorders and substance-related disorders frequently complicate the course of OCD
• The estimated interval between the onset of symptoms and the decision to seek help is between 5 and 10 years; the usual presentation is to a physician (other than a psychiatrist) for somatic complications (e.g. damaged skin from repeated hand washing)

Obsessive-Compulsive Disorder

Like delusions, obsessions tend to fall into a relatively small number of themes:

Theme	Corresponding Obsession
• cleanliness	• contamination
• order	• symmetry, precision
• sex & aggression	• assault, sexual assault, homicide, insults
• doubt	• safety, catastrophe, unworthiness

Another scheme for classifying obsessions is as follows:
• *Intellectual obsessions* – involving philosophical or metaphysical questions about life, the universe & everything; destiny; curved space; gravity waves, etc.
• *Inhibiting obsessions* – doubts or prohibitions about actions which may be harmful to others; the patient may become withdrawn or isolated to ensure such actions do not occur
• *Impulsive obsessions* – urges to steal, collect (hoard), or count (called arithomania)

Obsessions are also seen in:
• depression – obsessive thoughts about death, illness, a bleak future, self-deprecation, negative view of others, etc.
• psychotic disorders – the prodrome of schizophrenia can include obsessions, which cause the patient to perform unusual rituals
• other anxiety disorders – such as phobias, where the patient is tormented by thoughts of the feared object or situation when not faced with it
• Obsessive-Compulsive Personality Disorder (OCPD) – which shares some features with OCD (see also p. 130)
• Hypochondriasis – preoccupation with having a serious illness (p. 87)
• Body Dysmorphic Disorder – intrusive thoughts of a distorted self-image
• Impulse-Control Disorders (p. 96)
• partial complex seizure disorder (temporal lobe epilepsy)
• Tourette's disorder
• organic mental disorders – e.g. traumatic head injuries, carbon monoxide poisoning, disorders of the basal ganglia, cardiovascular accidents

• Preoccupations differ from obsessions in that they are a willful return to thinking or conversing about a topic (in a focused manner)
• Rumination is another term for an intellectual obsession; here, people "chew" (mull over) their "cud" (thoughts) without achieving a resolution; there is often an irritating and unnecessary quality (both in time and intensity) to this style of communicating

Obsessive-Compulsive Disorder

Practice Points

• Obsessions tend to fall within a small number of themes, with aggression, cleanliness, and order being the most prominent. In Freud's psychosexual stages of development, these are the issues that dominate the **anal phase**. Control and autonomy are the key outcomes from this stage. Freud linked obsessive behaviors to difficulties during the **anal stage** of development, and defined the **anal triad** as consisting of *parsimoniousness, orderliness,* and *obstinacy* (mnemonic – P.O.O.). The following ego defenses are thought to be operative in OCD:

• **Ambivalence** develops as a result of the simultaneous existence of longing (love) and aggressive wishes (hate). This conflict of opposing emotions paralyzes the patient with indecision, and results in the *doing-undoing* pattern seen with obsessions and compulsions.

• **Undoing** involves an action, either verbalization or behavior, that symbolically makes amends for conflicts, stresses, or unacceptable wishes. This is the predominant defense contributing to the compulsive component.

• **Magical Thinking** is also a component of OCD in that the obsession is given great power, and is seen to be more connected to events than is realistic.

• **Isolation (of affect)** separates or strips an idea from its accompanying feeling or affect. This is the predominant defense contributing to the obsessive component. An idea is made conscious, but the feelings are kept within the unconscious. When this defense is used to a lesser degree, three other mechanisms may be used:

> • intellectualization – excessive use of abstract thinking
> • moralization – morality isolates contradictory feelings
> • rationalization – justification of unacceptable attitudes

• **Reaction Formation** transforms an impulse into a diametrically opposed thought, feeling, or behavior. This is frequently seen as a "counter-dependent" attitude in which patients (primarily with obsessive-compulsive personalities) eradicate dependency on anyone or anything. Similarly, maintenance of a calm exterior will guard against an awareness of angry feelings. For example, orderliness is a reaction formation against the childhood desire to make a mess.

• **Displacement** redirects feelings from a conflict or stressor onto a symbolically related, but less threatening, person or object. "Kicking the dog" or "shooting the messenger" are examples of this defense.

Posttraumatic Stress Disorder

Posttraumatic Stress Disorder (**PTSD**) is a reaction to a severe stressor that is out of usual human experience. Frequently, the traumatic event is a war, assault, natural disaster, or accident. PTSD involves symptoms in each of 3 sets of reactions:
• Persistent re-experiencing of the event
• Avoidance of stimuli associated with the trauma
• Symptoms of increased arousal

Biological Features
• Hyperactivity of the hypothalamic-pituitary-adrenal axis
• Pathways from the locus ceruleus (noradrenergic transmission) mediate the symptoms of hyperarousal
• Temperamental/genetic factors influence the response to stress

Psychosocial Features
• PTSD has a prevalence of 1%; there are no gender differences
• This disorder is a combination of attempts to master the trauma through repetition and attempts to avoid such repetition
• The traumatic event may awaken previously unresolved conflicts and reactivate primitive instinctual drives

Biological Treatment
• There is no clear pharmacologic treatment of choice for PTSD
• Treatment of depression or anxiety symptoms is recommended
• Many other medications have been given anecdotal support

Psychosocial Treatment
• Cognitive-behavioral approaches have been established; the initial focus is on relaxation training; hypnosis is also used
• Psychodynamic approaches may involve **abreaction** of the event
• Education about PTSD (especially the risk of developing a substance-related disorder) and group therapy are helpful

Prognosis
• The prognosis is variable; over 75% of patients either recover or have mild symptoms; 10% have chronic severe symptoms
• The old and young tend to have a more complicated course
• Pre-existing psychiatric conditions worsen the prognosis

Posttraumatic Stress Disorder

"PRIDE AFRAID CHAINS"

Physiologic reactivity when exposed to cues
Recollections of the event that are distressing
Internal cues cause distress (symbolic reminders)
Dreams of the event that are distressing
External cues cause distress

} re-experi-ence of the event

Avoids stimuli associated with the trauma
Foreshortened future – has no long-term goals
Recall of the event is impaired
Affect has a restricted range
Interest in activities is diminished
Detached from others

} avoidance of stimuli

Concentration is impaired
Hypervigilance
Angry outbursts
Impairment in social and occupational functioning
Nocturnal problems – trouble falling asleep
　　　or staying asleep
Startle response – exaggerated reactions

} increased arousal symptoms

Practice Points
• The presence of emotional vulnerability or pre-existing psychopathology predisposes individuals to develop PTSD
• PTSD has historically been called Soldier's Heart, DaCosta's Heart (from a description of Civil War casualties), and Shell Shock
• The severity of the stressor does not necessarily correlate with symptom severity; the person's subjective response is the key
• PTSD must be present for at least one month to be diagnosed
• Symptoms lasting less than 4 weeks but at least 2 days, are diagnosed as an acute stress disorder

Generalized Anxiety Disorder

Generalized Anxiety Disorder (**GAD**) is characterized by excessive and pervasive worry accompanied by physical symptoms. The anxiety is not confined to the symptoms of another clinical disorder (e.g. being anxious about public speaking, as in social phobia).

Biological Features
• Genetic factors are not yet well understood in GAD
• There is both genetic and clinical evidence that MDD and GAD exist on a spectrum of expression; these disorders often co-exist
• Peripherally, anxiety is manifested by the sympathetic nervous system; in the CNS, the neurotransmitters involved are GABA, serotonin, norepinephrine, glutamate, and possibly others

Psychosocial Features
• GAD has a lifetime prevalence of 5%; women are diagnosed approximately twice as often as men
• Winnicott – failure of the parental holding environment
• Freud – anxiety is a signal to the ego that an instinctual urge is pressing for expression
• Stack Sullivan – anxiety stems from fear related to disapproval

Biological Treatment
• Site of action is a complex consisting of a benzodiazepine receptor, $GABA_A$ receptor and chloride channel; neuronal hyperpolarization reduces the firing rate and decreases anxiety
• Buspirone is indicated for GAD
• MAOIs, TCAs, antihistamines, and beta-blockers are also used

Psychosocial Treatment
• Cognitive-behavioral approaches have been established; the initial focus is on relaxation training (also biofeedback)
• Psychodynamic approaches search for the root of the anxiety

Prognosis
The prognosis for GAD depends on the presence of:
• Perpetuating factors – removing their influence improves outcome
• Comorbid conditions (e.g. MDD, panic disorder) – worsen the prognosis

Generalized Anxiety Disorder

"I'M A FICKLE CASE"

Impaired functioning (social, occupational, etc.)
Muscle tension

Axis I condition, if coexisting, is not the focus of the anxiety

Fatigued
Irritable
Control of worry is difficult
Keyed up (edgy)
Lasts for at least six months, occurs more days than not
Events and activities are focus of the worry (not just a single focus)

Concentration is impaired
Anxiety is excessive
Sleep disturbance
Excluded – substance disorders & general medical conditions

Practice Points
• GAD is often precipitated by a psychosocial stressor
• Buspirone appears to be less useful if benzodiazepines have been used recently
• The dexamethasone suppression test (**DST**) is often positive in GAD
• Cardiac, endocrine, and neurologic illnesses are among the most common medical causes of anxiety disorders
• Tolerance does not appear to develop to the anxiolytic effects of benzodiazepines; however, addiction is a long-term concern
• *Angst* is the German word for fear; the initial translations of Freud's work used it as a replacement for anxiety
• Freud used the term anxiety neurosis to refer to both GAD and panic disorder
• **Separation anxiety**, **castration anxiety**, and **superego anxiety** are important psychological factors in anxiety disorders

Somatization Disorder

Somatization disorder (**SD**) is characterized by multisystem physical complaints that cannot be explained medically. If a medical condition does exist, the symptoms are excessive for the degree of pathology present. This disorder is also called **Briquet's syndrome**.

Biological Features
• Male relatives of females with SD have an increased risk of antisocial personality disorder and substance-related disorders; female relatives have an increased prevalence of SD
• There may be alterations in the processing of information from somatic sources; "somatizing" patients may habitually focus on, and emphasize, minor physical sensations

Psychosocial Features
• Lifetime prevalence for women is 0.5%; SD is at least 5 times more common in women; cultural factors may influence development
• Childhood abuse may predispose to SD later in life
• Somatization is also an ego defense mechanism
• Somatization behavior may be a strategy to get attention that wouldn't otherwise be given for emotional problems

Biological Treatment
• Distinguishing medically explainable symptoms from somatized complaints is crucial; SD patients can develop serious illnesses
• Once the above distinction has been made, what is not done (i.e. investigations) is as important as what is done
• Depression and anxiety disorders are the two most common co-existing conditions that require pharmacologic treatment

Psychosocial Treatment
• Coordination by one physician is preferable
• Searching for the emotional component in symptom formation helps patients develop a vocabulary for expressing feelings

Prognosis
• SD is a chronic condition, and one of the few diagnoses with an age stipulation (onset prior to age 30); the course fluctuates, often with a change in symptoms instead of their disappearance

Somatization Disorder

"FOOT PAINS"

Four pain symptoms
One sexual symptom
One pseudoneurological symptom
Two gastrointestinal symptoms

Physical complaints are in excess of actual medical conditions
Age of onset under 30 years
Investigations do not reveal a cause for the complaints
Not due to malingering or factitious disorder
Social, occupational, or academic functioning is affected

Practice Points
• SD occurs more frequently in patients:
  • from lower socio-economic groups
  • with less education and intelligence
  • with avoidant, passive-aggressive, self-defeating, or obsessive-compulsive personality traits and disorders
• Involvement in a form of psychotherapy has been reported to lessen medical expenses by about half
• Societal roles or expectations may account for the gender discrepancy seen in SD; another hypothesis is that a common genotype or histrionic temperament is manifested as SD in women and antisocial personality disorder in men
• Another mnemonic for SD is based on 7 screening questions developed by Othmer & DeSouza*

• Shortness of breath (without exertion)	**S**omatization
• Dysmenorrhea	**D**isorder
• Burning in sexual organs or rectum	**B**esets
• Lump in throat	**L**adies
• Amnesia	**A**nd
• Vomiting	**V**exes
• Pain in the extremities	**P**hysicians

*Othmer, E. & DeSouza, C.: **A Screening Test for Somatization Disorder** *American Journal of* Psychiatry, 142 (10): p.1146–9, 1985

Conversion Disorder

"VIPERS"

Voluntary motor or sensory function is affected
Intentional production of symptoms is absent
Psychological factors are associated with onset of symptoms
Explanation of symptoms is not medically possible
Ruled out other disorders – pain, sexual dysfunction, etc.
Significant impairment in social or occupational functioning

Practice Points
• Conversion implies that an unconscious conflict is "converted" into physical symptoms, often with a symbolic connection to the conflict (for example, a wish to punch someone would be manifested as an inability to use the punching arm)
• The prevalence varies widely, but it is likely less than 1%
• Conversion disorder is more prevalent in patients with personality disorders, lower intelligence and education, and those suffering from chronic psychiatric illnesses
• **Primary gain** is the intrapsychic advantage achieved by keeping the conflict from conscious awareness; **secondary gain** is an external or "real world" advantage bestowed on the patient through removal from the precipitating situation; **tertiary gain** is the advantage that others get from the patient's secondary gain (e.g. supporting a whole family on social assistance)
• Patients frequently model their symptoms after an illness suffered by someone close to them (called **identification**)
• An **amytal interview** (intravenous barbiturate) can produce a temporary diminution of conversion symptoms
• Symptoms often abate within a few days without any specific treatment
• Many patients go on to develop clearly diagnosable neurological conditions in the future
• Conversion disorder can present with motor symptoms, sensory symptoms, seizures, or any combination of these

Hypochondriasis

"DRIPS"

Delusional intensity of thoughts is not present
Reassurance does not lessen the patient's concern
Impairment in social or occupational functioning is present
Preoccupation with the idea of having a serious illness
Six-month minimum duration

Hypochondriasis is the persistent fear of being afflicted with a serious illness. The fear is unfounded, and based on a misinterpretation of bodily symptoms. The term means "below the ribs" and was so named due to the frequency of GI complaints.

Practice Points
• Hypochondriacal patients may have a constitutional sensitivity to somatic symptoms (e.g. a low pain threshold)
• While hypochondriasis is listed as an ego defense, it can be broken down into the components of **repression** (which keeps the conflict from awareness) and **displacement** (which shifts the focus from the target of the conflict someplace else, in this case, it is back onto the patient)
• Hypochondriasis can be thought of as an internal "death sentence" for the guilt felt over aggressive impulses towards another person; it may also serve as a mechanism of atonement for an unacceptable impulse or act*
• Hypochondriasis can be considered a disorder of perception*
• Depression and/or anxiety disorders frequently coexist
• Examples of general medical conditions that can be confused with hypochondriasis are occult neoplasms, multiple sclerosis, myasthenia gravis, and connective tissue disorders with multi-system involvement (in order to decrease the amount of egg worn on one's face, a thorough investigation is warranted)
• Treatment usually involves an agreement to coordinate treatment with one doctor who can limit referrals and tests; patients may be interested in groups that focus on chronic illness

* Thanks to **Dr. John Mount** of London, Ontario for his teaching in this area

Factitious Disorder

The hallmark of Factitious Disorder (**FD**) is the conscious production of symptoms in order to "assume the sick role." The goal appears to be hospital admission, and to be the focus of clinical investigation and treatment. It is both a fascinating and disturbing disorder. FD is of particular interest in psychiatry, both because of the interest in human motivation and because the symptoms that make up the diagnostic criteria can be faked (sometimes with incredible accuracy). FD does not appear to be explainable on the basis of an obvious gain. For example, opioid (narcotic) medications can be relatively easily obtained – one needn't be admitted to a hospital solely to obtain them.

Patients often have some familiarity with healthcare terminology and procedures, and know which symptoms to emphasize. They are often eager to have invasive procedures performed – possibly in the hope that a complication develops or a coincidental finding is made. The etiology of this disorder remains obscure, but clearly involves profound disturbances in identity and personality formation. This disorder has also been called **Münchausen's syndrome**, which is a misnomer because he was more of a raconteur than someone fabricating a serious illness. Other terms used are **hospital addiction** and **pseudologia fantastica**. Management involves early detection, limiting investigations, and avoiding unnecessary medication.

Malingering

Malingering is the conscious production of symptoms for an obvious gain (called **secondary gain**). It is not considered a mental disorder. Common types of secondary gain involve: diminution of responsibility for legal or financial problems; prescription medication abuse; avoiding military service; being relieved of unpleasant responsibilities; disability income; admission to hospital, etc. A method for distinguishing among these disorders is as follows:

Disorder	Secondary Gain	Conscious Production
Conversion Disorder	–	–
Factitious Disorder	–	+
Malingering	+	+

Dissociative Identity Disorder

Multiple Personality Disorder (**MPD**) was renamed Dissociative Identity Disorder (**DID**) in the DSM-IV. The essential feature is the co-existence of two or more distinct identities or personalities that take control of an individual and cause deficits in the recall of his or her activities.

Historically, DID has been classified as hysterical neuroses, dissociative type. Renaming this condition emphasizes the psychological process producing the different identities (dissociation), rather than the observable manifestations (multiple personalities). Additionally, it implies that a single person manifests different internal and external experiences of "self."

There can be a fascinating variability observed in the "alters," which can be sufficiently well defined to be considered separate "personalities." The alters can have distinct: names; sexual identities and orientation; voices; facility with foreign languages; handedness and handwriting. Amazingly, each can have distinct illnesses, EEGs, eyeglass prescriptions, and even allergies!

The usual arrangement involves a dominant personality that is aware of all of the fragments, though this is not usually the personality that seeks treatment. Alters appear to be variably aware of one another. The total number of personalities in some reports exceeds 50, with the average being in the range of 10 to 12. Frequently, the personalities have some connection with one another. For example, all of the persons involved in a traumatic episode (victim, perpetrator, witness, etc.) can be embodied by different personalities. Also, dichotomous personalities (e.g. a good-evil pairing) are often present. The duality of human nature has often been portrayed using multiple personality themes. A classic example is Robert Louis Stevenson's *Dr. Jekyll and Mr. Hyde*, which has been made into several movie versions. Films have also been made from real cases, in particular *The Three Faces of Eve* and *Sybil*.

Anorexia Nervosa

The hallmark of Anorexia Nervosa (**AN**) is a refusal to maintain a weight of at least 85% of that expected (by age and height) on normal growth curves. Patients with AN have an intense fear of gaining weight due to a distorted perception of their body image.

Biological Features
• The physical effects are identical to those seen with starvation
• May be genetically linked to mood disorders and substance abuse

Psychosocial Features
• AN is more common in developed countries, and is 15 times more common in females; the prevalence is about 0.5%
• Patients may strive for autonomy and independence from parents who are (or are perceived to be) over-controlling
• AN fosters the regression to a pre-pubescent state where the demands and expectations of adulthood are not present

Biological Treatment
• Hospitalization may be necessary to prevent death from dehydration, electrolyte disturbances, or cardiac arrhythmias
• The possible role of endogenous opioids in maintaining a state of starvation has prompted the use of opiate antagonists
• Antidepressants, neuroleptics, and cyproheptadine are used

Psychosocial Treatment
• Behavioral Management/Modification with family therapy and psychoeducation on an inpatient unit is a common starting point
• Patients are usually secretive about their exercising, vomiting, and unusual eating habits; meals in a group setting and restricting access to washrooms afterwards inhibits many behaviors
• Outpatient cognitive, psychodynamic, and family therapy is used

Prognosis
• The prognosis for AN is generally unfavorable; preoccupation with food persists even at a normal body weight
• Mortality rates are in excess of 10% for patients who do not achieve a normal body weight
• Overall psychosocial adjustment tends to remain compromised

Anorexia Nervosa

"I FEAR LARD"

Image of body is distorted – an abnormality of perception

Fear of gaining weight is intense
Expected weight gains are not made
Amenorrhea – 3 consecutive menstrual cycles missed
Refusal to gain weight

Laxative use – (characteristic of the binge eating/purging type)
Anhedonia – high prevalence of mood symptoms
Restricting Type
Denial – of weight loss or emaciated body shape

Practice Points
• "Anorexia" is a misnomer for this condition; appetite is usually not lost – patients willfully restrict their food intake
• Patients often have an intense interest in food, and cook elaborate meals for others, exchange recipes, etc.
• AN has many components of an obsessive-compulsive disorder regarding food (obsession) and weight loss (compulsion)
• Patients are adept at hiding food; it is frequently cut into small pieces or concealed to give the illusion of consumption
• Quantities of food are often sequestered in hiding places, carried in clothing or purses, or are stolen on impulse from stores
• Aside from the perceptual aberration regarding body shape, the MSE is usually unremarkable
• More than half of patients retain abnormal eating patterns or develop chronic anorexia; poor prognosis factors include:
  • comorbid bulimia nervosa
  • binge eating/purging type
  • mood disorder or OCD co-existing with AN
  • older age of onset
  • poor premorbid adjustment
  • coexisting general medical conditions
  • severe somatic complications
  • lack of social supports

Bulimia Nervosa

The hallmark of Bulimia Nervosa (**BN**) is recurrent ingestion of large quantities of food (binge eating), over which patients feel they lack a sense of control. Subsequently, there is a dysphoric state (guilt, disgust, depression – the so-called "post-binge anguish"), which is followed by some type of compensation for the high caloric intake.

Biological Features
• Several medical complications can occur with BN
• BN may have a connection to mood disorders, impulse-control disorders, and borderline personality disorder

Psychosocial Features
• BN is more common than AN; the female/male ratio is 10:1
• Psychodynamic factors are thought to be similar to AN; parents may be (or be seen as) more neglectful than controlling
• Bulimic patients lack superego control and externalize their conflicts with impulsive and self-damaging behavior (promiscuity, shoplifting, substance abuse, suicide attempts, etc.)

Biological Treatment
• Hospitalization is not needed as frequently as with AN
• Use of antidepressants is indicated; several have shown efficacy (particularly fluoxetine, and also MAOIs, TCAs) independent of the presence of a mood disorder; mood stabilizers have also been used

Psychosocial Treatment
• Psychotherapy (cognitive-behavioral, psychodynamic or family) on an outpatient basis suffices for most patients
• Comorbidity with other conditions makes this a challenging disorder to treat; BN often requires prolonged therapy

Prognosis
• The prognosis for BN is generally better than for AN; a typical course is that of waxing and waning; at the five-year point, one-third are doing well, one-third have some symptoms, and one-third do poorly
• Occasional binge eating has been reported in almost half of college-age women; this appears to spontaneously remit in most cases without further episodes or complications

Bulimia Nervosa

"A BINGE"

Average of 2 binges/week over 3 months

Behavior after consumption compensates for ingestion*
Ingestion of large amounts of food (binge eating)
Not occurring exclusively during anorexia nervosa
Guilty feelings after binge eating
Evaluation of self is unduly based on appearance

* Laxatives, cathartics, diuretics, self-induced vomiting, exercise, and surreptitious use of thyroid medication are methods used to compensate for the huge caloric load caused by binge eating

Practice Points
• Bulimia Nervosa is divided into *purging* and *nonpurging types*
• A history of pica (eating of non-nutritive substances such as hair or mud) may be present in bulimic patients
• AN and BN patients tend to be high achievers who are concerned with trying to be "perfect" – including body image
• Bulimic patients tend to have better social and sexual adjustment than patients with AN
• The body weight of most BN patients is in the normal range
• Often the texture and consistency of foods make them appealing; popular favorites are smooth, creamy and sweet foods such as pudding, whipped cream, or the filling in an Oreo® cookie

Important medical considerations are:
• **Kleine-Levin syndrome** (hyperphagia and hypersomnia over a period of weeks, often seen in adolescents, course is self-limiting)
• **Klüver-Bucy syndrome**, which results from limbic system dysfunction, and consists of: visual and auditory agnosia, placidity, hyperorality (exploring items by mouth), hypersexuality, and hyperphagia; this can be seen in: Pick's disease, HIV encephalopathy, herpes encephalitis, brain tumors, etc.

Adjustment Disorder

An Adjustment Disorder (**AD**) is a time-limited, maladaptive response to an upsetting event (called a **psychosocial stressor**) that is out of proportion to what would be reasonably expected. AD causes significant impairment in an individual's ability to function socially or at work. There are time constraints involved in this diagnosis:
• Symptoms occur within 3 months of the onset of the stressor
• Remission occurs within 6 months of the termination of the stressor, or the consequences of the stressor

AD is not diagnosed if the symptoms can be better explained as an exacerbation of a pre-existing illness. Additionally, symptoms are not severe enough to qualify for the diagnosis of PTSD.

Biological Features
• Vegetative signs can be seen when depressed mood is the predominant symptom; physical signs of anxiety can also be seen
• AD can lead to other physical difficulties, such as exacerbation of pre-existing medical illnesses (e.g. cardiac and gastrointestinal)
• Substance-related disorders can develop as a reaction to AD

Psychosocial Features
• AD is common, and is present in up to 20% of inpatients
• The nature of the stressor and its significance to the patient (actual and symbolic) are key considerations
• A patient's previous reaction to stressful situations provides a guide to what may be required to manage the current situation

Biological Treatment
• Antidepressants and anxiolytics may be required

Psychosocial Treatment
• Psychotherapy is the treatment of choice; it can reduce the reaction to the current stressor and decrease recurrences

Prognosis
• The overall outcome is quite favorable; the vast majority of patients resume their previous level of functioning; mood, anxiety, or substance-related disorders worsen the prognosis

Adjustment Disorder

"IT'S BAD"

Impairment of social, occupational, academic functioning
Three-month (or less) onset of symptoms from time of stressor
Six-month (or less) duration of symptoms from end of stressor

Bereavement has been excluded
Another (**A**xis I) diagnosis is excluded
Distress is beyond expectation for the stressor involved

Practice Points
• AD is a diagnosis of exclusion after other Axis I & II disorders have been considered first
• Subtypes of AD are:
> • with depressed mood
> • with anxiety
> • with mixed anxiety and depressed mood
> • with disturbance of conduct
> • with mixed disturbance of emotions and conduct
> • unspecified

• Uncomplicated bereavement involves an expectable reaction to a loss; AD involves a reaction in excess of that which is expected
• PTSD involves stressors beyond the range of usual human experiences
• Patients with personality disorders or cognitive disorders are prone to develop AD
• Brief therapy and crisis intervention are useful psychotherapies for treating AD
• The DSM-IV contains research diagnoses for conditions called *Minor Depressive Disorder* and *Recurrent Brief Depressive Disorder* in Appendix B; should these conditions be adopted as formal diagnoses, many patients currently diagnosed with *Adjustment Disorder with Depressed Mood* will receive these diagnoses instead
• AD used to be called a *Transient Situational Disturbance* or a *Transient Situational Personality Disorder*

Impulse-Control Disorders

Impulse-Control Disorders are listed separately in the DSM-IV. They consist of behaviors with the following common elements:
• An urge, impulse, or temptation that is too strong to resist
• The resulting action harms the person, someone else, or property
• An increasing degree of tension is experienced before the act
• There is a release of tension and gratification during the act
• The act is not committed for an obvious goal, such as needing to eat, revenge, dire financial circumstances, etc.

The impulses can be conscious or unconscious. Some patients experience remorse for their actions, but at the time, the impulse is carried out in an ego-syntonic manner (i.e. it doesn't distress the patient, see also p. 112). Psychosocial theories postulate a fixation at Freud's **oral stage** of development. These individuals are needy or "hungry" and may engage in these behaviors to get attention and perhaps love from others. Another possibility is that these actions mediate strong feelings of depression, anxiety, or guilt.

Biological theories focus on the similarities between impulsivity and temporal lobe epilepsy. Additionally, patients with head trauma, mental retardation, and attention-deficit/hyperactivity disorder seem to manifest these behaviors more frequently. Decreased levels of serotonin and its metabolites have been correlated with violent acts.

A mnemonic for the five impulse-control disorders is as follow:

"Kick-In-The Pants Psychotherapy"

Kleptomania
Intermittent Explosive Disorder
Trichotillomania
Pyromania
Pathological Gambling

In the above illustration, the impulse-control disorders are (from left to right): pathological gambling, kleptomania, pyromania, trichotillomania, and intermittent explosive disorder

Practice Points

Pathological Gambling

• A support group called Gamblers Anonymous (GA) is available
• Many of the predisposing factors for depression are also seen in this disorder (e.g. loss of a parent, divorce, poverty, harsh discipline, etc.)

Kleptomania

• Kleptomanic patients are compelled to commit the act of theft; they do not have a use or need for the stolen object, and often have enough money to have purchased the item
• Kleptomania is unplanned, and almost always a solitary act
• Theft of items can be a feature of schizophrenia, bulimia nervosa, mania, and antisocial or borderline personality disorders
• An old Rodney Dangerfield joke: "My doctor diagnosed me with kleptomania – he said I should take something for it."

Pyromania

• Cruelty to animals, truancy, delinquency, and enuresis are common historical features; these patients are almost exclusively male
• There is often a fascination with fire, fire-fighting equipment, and flammable compounds
• No obvious gain exists for the person to set the fire

Trichotillomania

• Human hair is a remarkably resilient substance, and if swallowed can form a **bezoar** which can lead to intestinal obstruction
• Trichotillomania has many features in common with OCD
• Many medications and therapies have been tried for this disorder

Intermittent Explosive Disorder

• Intermittent Explosive Disorder (**IED**) often involves a stressor that causes the patient to feel helpless, useless, or frustrated
• The resulting physical outburst is far out of proportion to the stressor, and the recall of the episode is frequently poor
• The patient's personality is not otherwise aggressive
• The personal history often reveals early deprivation, a violent caregiver, and substance abuse by a parent or caregiver
• Predisposing factors also include head trauma, cerebral infections, or ADHD; soft neurologic signs and EEG changes are often present
• Treatment options include lithium, carbamazepine, dilantin, and SSRIs

8. Personality Disorders

Personality or personality disorder?

Axis II

For a review of DSM-IV axes, check pages 3 and 4. The features of Axis II presented in this chapter are:
• Ego Defense Mechanisms
• Personality Disorders

Ego Defense Mechanisms

In order to more fully understand personality disorders, it is important to first have some facility with the concept of ego defenses.

Freud developed his **topographical theory** which divided the mind into the conscious, unconscious, and preconscious. The unconscious mind contains wishes seeking fulfillment that are closely related to instinctual drives, specifically sexual and aggressive urges. A type of thinking called **primary process** is associated with the unconscious. Primary process is not bound by logic, permits contradictions to coexist, contains no negatives, has no regard for time, and is highly symbolized. This is seen in dreams, psychosis, and children's thinking. The preconscious (thoughts or memories readily brought into awareness) and conscious mind use **secondary process** thinking. This is logical and deals with the demands of external reality. Secondary process is the goal-directed day-to-day type of thinking that adults use.

Over time, Freud incorporated his findings into a new **structural theory**, which was a model containing the **id**, **ego**, and **superego**. Present from birth, the id is completely unconscious and seeks gratification of instinctual (sexual and aggressive) drives. The superego forms from an identification with the same-sex parent at the resolution of the **oedipal conflict**. It suppresses instinctual aims, serves as the moral conscience in dictating what *should not* be done, and, as the ego ideal, dictates what *should* be done. The ego is the mediator between two sets of entities: the id and superego; and the person and reality. A fundamental concept in ego psychology is one of *conflict* among the id, ego, and superego as they battle for the expression and discharge of drives. This conflict produces anxiety, specifically called **signal anxiety**. This anxiety alerts the ego that a defense mechanism is required, which is one of the unconscious roles of the ego.

Ego Defenses Illustrated

Repression

Repression is considered to be the principal ego defense (and therefore deserves a large illustration). This defense involves an active process of excluding distressing material from conscious awareness, which Freud thought was integral to the formation of psychological symptoms. The "distressing material" can be further defined as consisting of an instinctual impulse, an idea, and the accompanying emotion (called **affect**). For an example, let's get oedipal. A boy may consciously be aware of hating his father; an idea and emotion which are both too upsetting for him to bear. If the idea re-enters consciousness, it may be altered so that rather than the father being hated, a substitute is used (such as another authority figure). In this way, what is forgotten is not forgotten, and the object of the strong feelings is symbolically linked to the original conflict.

Primary repression refers to stopping an idea or affect before it reaches consciousness. **Secondary repression** removes from consciousness what was once experienced.

Suppression is the conscious avoidance of attending to an impulse or conflict. For example, primary repression would involve not reading this page in the first place. Secondary repression would be reading it and then forgetting what was presented. Suppression would be consciously avoiding this book because it reminds you of an unpleasant event (like an upcoming examination).

Acting Out

Acting out involves the expression of unconscious impulses through behavior in order to avoid experiencing painful feelings. The action provides partial gratification of the wish rather than the prohibition against it. For example, as a patient in psychotherapy nears the end of treatment, unconscious fears of abandonment stemming from previous relationships arise. The patient may then "act out" by taking an overdose rather than dealing with the pain of feeling rejected. The action serves as a substitute for remembering and is an unrecognized (unconscious) repetition of earlier behavior. Acting out entails more than a single thought or behavior. The term is properly used to describe an inappropriate response to a current situation as if it were the original one causing the conflict. The term is often improperly used to describe conscious, impulsive behavior. This is more appropriately called **acting up** or misbehaving.

Controlling

Controlling is the unconscious manipulation of events, people, or objects in the environment to serve an inner need, such as reducing tension or lessening the anxiety accompanying a conflict or conflicted wish.

Dissociation

Dissociation is the sudden and drastic alteration of an aspect of consciousness, identity, or behavior. It is a temporary state which allows the person to avoid emotional distress.

Identification

In this defense mechanism, patients adopt some, many, or all of the characteristics of another person as their own. As an example, this mechanism is familiar in the marketing of sports equipment in that the buyer identifies with the professionals who use (or at least endorse) the brand.

Displacement

Displacement transfers the emotion attached to a conflicted wish or relationship to one where expression is permitted, more acceptable, or at least less forbidden. Common examples are "kicking the dog" or "shooting the messenger." The target of the discharge remains symbolically linked to the original source of the conflict.

Introjection

This defense involves internalizing the image or qualities of a person (usually a parent or other significant figure).

Distortion

This involves altering one's perception of the environment by replacing reality with a more acceptable version in order to suit inner needs. The degree of distortion can be mild or can be so severe that psychosis develops.

Idealization/Devaluation

In **idealization**, exceedingly positive qualities (e.g. beauty, strength, skill) are ascribed to another person. Typically, the object of the idealization demonstrates the desirable qualities to some extent, and is someone who can provide comfort, assistance, empathy, etc., but not to the (unrealistic) level desired by the patient. If such wishes are met to a cer-

tain extent, this only serves to increase expectations, escalating to the point where the idealized person cannot possibly meet them. Inevitably, disappointment results, whereby the idealized person is **devalued** far out of proportion to the actual "failure." An example of this is the hero worship lavished on movie stars or athletes. They can do no wrong until they snub you for an autograph or don't reply to your tenth fan letter, at which point they plummet to a place beneath contempt.

Inhibition

Inhibition is an unconscious confinement or restraining of instinctual impulses. Here, the superego prevents the expression of an impulse from the id. Inhibition has also been described as a conscious mechanism which serves the similar purpose of helping avoid expression of the conflicted wish, which would cause problems with the superego (conscience) and/or other people.

Intellectualization

This defense involves the extreme or exclusive use of "thinking" to deal with emotional issues. This has also been referred to as a "thinking compulsion." Attention is focused on external matters, inanimate objects, or irrelevant details to avoid intimacy. Expression of emotion is restricted. This is present in an unempathic "just deal with it" attitude, and is a component of brooding where events are continually rehashed in a distant, abstract, emotionally barren fashion.

Isolation of Affect

This defense, which is also simply called **isolation**, involves the separation of an idea and its accompanying affect. The affect is subsequently kept out of conscious awareness. The idea, stripped of its emotional charge, is more easily dealt with on a conscious level.

Passive-Aggression

Passive-aggressive behavior refers to the expression of hostile feelings in a non-confrontational manner. Examples are lateness, procrastination, telling partial truths, and acts of omission rather than commission. The passive and aggressive elements are expressed simultaneously. This term was applied to a discrete personality disorder in the DSM-III-R, and was deleted presumably because these forms of behavior are so common they couldn't properly be considered a disorder.

Projection

Projection involves the casting out or "projecting" onto others the thoughts or feelings that a person cannot tolerate as being his or her own. In the example shown, the man with the glasses blames his wife for having an affair with the elderly gentleman, when he himself has been harboring yearnings for another woman. This can also be summed up as, "a good defense starts with a good offense." By blaming others for their sentiments and actions, the focus stays away from the person doing the accusing.

Splitting

This defense divides external objects into all-good or all-bad categories. Ambivalence towards the external object is not possible. Rapid shifts between these categories is also seen, with little to no recall of the previous view or awareness of the self-contradictory switch. Splitting can be directed towards a single person, group of people, institutions, etc. Often only a minor or symbolic event produces a shift in the split.

Projective Identification

Projective identification is difficult to conceptualize. A quick analogy is that of a *self-fulfilling prophecy*. Here, unwanted aspects of the self are "projected" onto others, and in a way that somehow applies to them. In the illustration on the next page, the patient can't tolerate feelings of being unlikable, so via projection, the therapist is accused of hating her. This projection is "reasonable" because some patients are difficult to work with, and in this instance there may have been an initial reaction that felt like rejection to the patient. The patient then exerts interpersonal pressure on the therapist to think and feel in a way that is in accordance with the projection. Finally, once this projection is "processed" by the therapist, it is reinternalized by the patient, and in this case, she makes herself into a difficult patient. This defense is effective in making others feel what the patient is experiencing herself.

Rationalization

Rationalization is the process of covering up unreasonable or unacceptable acts and ideas with seemingly reasonable explanations. Justification is provided for beliefs or behaviors that would otherwise appear illogical, irrational, or immoral.

Reaction Formation

In this defense, unacceptable wishes are transformed into their complete opposite. This has also been called **reversal formation**, and can be thought of as socializing the infantile urges that persist on an unconscious level.

Regression

Regression involves the return to a previous (earlier) level of functioning to serve the purpose of conflict avoidance. It is easier to find gratification at earlier stages of development, and it entails fewer responsibilities. Regression can be seen to an extent in many inpatients who, because of illness, cannot maintain their usual level of function, and have fewer expectations placed on them while in hospital.

Schizoid Fantasy

Fantasy is used as an escape and as a means of gratification whereby other people are not required for emotional fulfillment. The retreat into fantasy itself acts as a means of distancing others.

Sexualization

Here, objects, situations, and people are colored with sexual overtones that were either not there initially, or if present, were subtle. This can help lessen anxiety by reducing everything to a base level, or assigning a common element to unknown or uncomfortable situations.

Somatization

In this defense, psychological difficulties become expressed as physical complaints. There is also a major psychiatric (Axis I) condition called **somatization disorder** (p. 84). Somatization is considered a form of regression because expressing somatic problems verbally is a progressive step. Some family situations and cultures encourage somatization because little attention gets paid to emotional concerns, thereby encouraging their expression in physical terms.

Undoing

Undoing is an action instead of a psychological mechanism. The behavior is linked to the conflict, and is carried out to prevent or reverse the consequences that are anticipated from the impulse. Undoing can be realistically or magically associated with the conflict and serves to reduce anxiety and control the underlying impulse (e.g. avoiding sidewalk cracks so as to not break one's mother's back).

Denial

In this defense reality is simply ignored. Painful affects or memories are avoided by the disavowal of sensory input. Denial can be a primitive defense, but it also has adaptive elements and can be useful in coping with serious conditions or traumatic events.

Mature Ego Defenses

The preceding section is not a comprehensive presentation of ego defenses, but an introduction to those that are relevant in this chapter. Everyone uses defense mechanisms to some extent because they help the ego function. For example, some patients with terminal illnesses fare better with a moderate amount of denial regarding their medical condition. **Regression** is an essential ingredient in creativity, and the term **regression in service of the ego** refers to instances where it is beneficial to allow one's self to enjoy a less demanding situation or experience. Mature ego defenses allow the expression of impulses in socially acceptable ways.

Sublimation

This defense allows the channeling of aggressive impulses towards a modified outlet. Sports, particularly those involving body contact, are an example of expressed sublimated urges.

Anticipation

Anticipation involves the postponement of wishes or impulses until they can be more appropriately expressed. Discomfort may result from deferring action, but satisfaction is achieved from avoiding unpleasant outcomes.

Ego Defenses

"BUD HAS PRICE"

Blocking
Undoing
Displacement, **D**enial, **D**istortion, **D**issociation

Hypochondriasis, **H**umor
Acting Out, **A**ltruism, **A**nticipation, **A**sceticism
Sublimation, **S**uppression, **S**chizoid Fantasy, **S**omatization

Projection, **P**rojective Identification, **P**assive-Aggressive Behavior,
      Primitive Idealization
Rationalization, **R**eaction Formation, **R**epression, **R**egression
Identification, **I**dealization, **I**ntrojection, **I**nhibition,
      Intellectualization, **I**solation of Affect
Controlling
Externalization

Practice Points
• Ego defense mechanisms are unconscious processes recruited in response to an internal or external threat; repression is the primary defense and others are used when it becomes overwhelmed
• Personality disorders can be characterized by which ego defenses are used, and the extent to which they are used
• The following are considered conscious roles of the ego
    • perception (sense of reality)
    • reality testing (adaptation to reality)
    • motor control
    • intuition
    • memory
    • affect
    • thinking (the ego uses **secondary process**) and learning
    • control of instinctual drives (delay of immediate gratification)
    • synthetic functions (assimilation, creation, coordination)
    • language and comprehension

Ego Defenses in Personality Disorders

Personalities become "disordered" by the maladaptive use of ego defenses, both in terms of which defenses are used, and the extent to which they are used. A more detailed account of these defenses is contained in major reference texts (see the *References* and *Recommended Reading Sections*).

The primary ego defenses used in the different personality disorders are as follows:

Antisocial   Acting Out, Controlling, Dissociation, Projective Identification

Avoidant   Inhibition, Isolation, Displacement, Projection

Borderline   Splitting, Distortion, Acting Out, Dissociation, Projective Identification

Dependent   Idealization, Reaction Formation, Projective Identification, Inhibition, Somatization, Regression

Histrionic   Sexualization, Repression, Denial, Regression, Dissociation

Narcissistic   Idealization/Devaluation, Projection, Identification

Obsessive-Compulsive   Intellectualization, Undoing, Displacement, Isolation of Affect, Rationalization

Paranoid   Projection, Projective Identification, Denial, Splitting, Reaction Formation

Schizoid   Schizoid Fantasy, Intellectualization, Introjection, Projection, Idealization/Devaluation

Schizotypal   Projection, Denial, Distortion, Idealization, Schizoid Fantasy

Overview of Personality Disorders

A definition of **personality** is: *a relatively stable and enduring set of characteristic behavioral and emotional traits*. Over time, a person will interact with others in reasonably predictable ways. However, as the adage "don't judge a book by its cover" warns, circumstances can alter behavior so that someone does something "out of character." For example, extreme circumstances like divorce or New Year's Eve can bring out behavior that is atypical for that person.

A **personality disorder** is a variant, or an extreme set of characteristics, going beyond the range found in most people. The DSM-IV (p. 629) defines a personality disorder as "*An enduring pattern of inner experience and behavior that deviates markedly from the expectations of the individual's culture, is pervasive and inflexible, has an onset in adolescence or early adulthood, is stable over time, and leads to distress or impairment.*"

While many other definitions exist, features consistently emphasized in defining a personality disorder are that it:
• Is deeply ingrained and has an inflexible nature
• Is maladaptive, especially in interpersonal contexts
• Is relatively stable over time
• Significantly impairs the ability of the person to function

Personality disorders are **egosyntonic**, meaning that behaviors do not distress the person directly, but make more of an impact on those close to the person.

The criteria for diagnosing personality disorders are very much within the realm of common human experience. Each one of us at times has been or felt: hypervigilant, destructive, suspicious, shy, bossy, vain, striving for perfection, dramatic, afraid to be alone, fearful of rejection, purposely late for something, too independent, too needy, critical of others, resentful of authority, averse to criticism, bored, seductive, or undergone rapidly shifting emotional states.

None of these behaviors alone warrants the diagnosis of a personality disorder. Instead, clusters of behaviors existing over a lengthy time period and interfering with a person's ability to function make a diagnosis.

The DSM-IV divides personality disorders into three **clusters** based on descriptive or phenomenologic similarities:

Cluster A — Odd or Eccentric ("Mad")
    Paranoid, Schizoid, Schizotypal

Cluster B — Dramatic, Emotional or Erratic ("Bad")
    Antisocial, Borderline, Histrionic, Narcissistic

Cluster C — Anxious or Fearful ("Sad")
    Avoidant, Dependent, Obsessive-Compulsive

The diagnosis of **Personality Change Due to a Medical Condition** is made when a personality disturbance is due to the direct physiologic effects of a medical condition. This personality change must be a clear and persistent change from previous patterns.
• Common manifestations are: aggression, lability, apathy, suspiciousness, poor judgment, or impulsivity
• When this is given as the diagnosis, it is coded on Axis I as: "Personality Change Due to (Medical Condition)" – with the medical condition specified on Axis III

The paranoid, schizoid, schizotypal, and antisocial PDs are not diagnosed if they are coincident with certain Axis I conditions. Exclusion criteria are not listed for the other personality disorders. The antisocial personality disorder is the only diagnosis with an age requirement and a prerequisite diagnosis. Patients must be at least age eighteen, and have met the criteria for a diagnosis of conduct disorder before age fifteen (see p. 114 – 117). Personality disorders are not diagnosed exclusive of one another. In practice, there is usually one disorder that is more prominent, and this is recorded as the Axis II diagnosis, with the others listed as "features." If two or more are equally apparent, then all applicable diagnoses are recorded. The residual personality diagnosis in the DSM-IV is called **Personality Disorder Not Otherwise Specified (NOS)**. This is used when the patient does not meet the complete criteria for a single personality disorder, but exhibits individual diagnostic criteria from a variety of personality disorders. Additionally, if the criteria are met for the depressive or passive-aggressive (negativistic) personality disorders (considered research diagnoses in the DSM-IV), the diagnosis of **Personality Disorder NOS** is used.

Antisocial Personality Disorder
"CALLOUS MAN"

Conduct disorder before age 15y;
    Current age at least 18y
Antisocial acts; commits acts that
    are grounds for **A**rrest
Lies frequently
Lacunae – **L**acks a superego
Obligations not honored
Unstable – can't plan ahead
Safety of self and others ignored

Money problems – spouse and
    children are not supported
Aggressive, **A**ssaultive
Not occurring exclusively during schizophrenia or mania

Essence of the Antisocial Personality
"A pervasive pattern of disregard for, and violation of, the rights of others." (DSM-IV, 1994)

Ego Defenses
- Controlling
- Acting Out
- Projective Identification
- Dissociation

Practice Points
- The Antisocial Personality Disorder (ASPD) is also called the **sociopathic** or **psychopathic** personality

- A seminal book on this personality disorder is called: *The Mask of Sanity** by Dr. Hervey Cleckley (who also co-authored *The Three Faces of Eve*).
 * The *Mask of Sanity, Fifth Edition* is available from:
    Emily S. Cleckley, Publisher
    3024 Fox Spring Road
    Augusta, Georgia, U.S.A. 30909

Differential Diagnosis

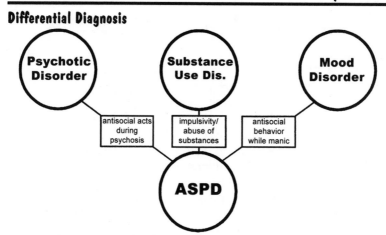

Antisocial Personality Themes

In addition to the diagnostic criteria, the following features become evident in the interview and history:

- Glibness, shallow emotion
- Requires constant stimulation
- Criminal "versatility"
- Parole/probation violations
- Promiscuity
- Juvenile delinquency
- Grandiosity
- Poor impulse control
- Avoids responsibility for actions
- Abuse of substances
- Superior physical prowess
- Behavioral problems as a child
- Social "parasites" – may have several sources of income: "under the table" cash, profit from stolen property or drugs, disability benefits, embezzlement, fraud, etc.

Practice Points

- Soft (non-localizing) neurological signs are often present:
- persistence of primitive reflexes: palmar-mental, grasp, etc.
- impaired coordination, gait, balance and motor performance
- graphesthesia, dysdiadochokinesis impaired; + Romberg sign
- ASPD appears to be genetically related to alcoholism and is frequently complicated by alcohol abuse
- Several factors in childhood are thought to be etiologically significant in the development of ASPD:
    - frequent moves, losses, family break-ups; large families
    - poverty, urban setting, poorly regulated schooling
    - indulgence of material needs, deprivation of emotional needs
    - enuresis, firesetting, and cruelty to animals

Cleckley's Psychopathic Personality Features

- Superficial charm and good "intelligence"
- Absence of delusions and other signs of irrational thinking
- Absence of "nervousness" or psychoneurotic manifestations
- Inadequately motivated antisocial behavior
- Poor judgment and failure to learn from experience
- Pathologic egocentricity and incapacity for love
- General poverty in major affective reactions
- Unresponsiveness in general interpersonal relations
- Fantastic and inviting behavior with drink and sometimes without
- Sex life impersonal, trivial, and poorly integrated
- Suicide rarely carried out
- Failure to follow any life plan
- Unreliability
- Untruthfulness and insincerity
- Lack of remorse or shame
- Specific loss of insight

Source: Cleckley (1988). Reprinted with permission.

 **Practice Points**

A key diagnostic point is that not all criminal behavior is due to ASPD, and not all ASPDs commit chargeable offenses. A proper evaluation requires a longitudinal history, with an understanding of the patient's interpersonal behavior. The main diagnostic criterion for ASPD is a pervasive and long-standing disregard for the rights of others, with unlawful behaviors being the usual (but not exclusive) manifestation. ASPDs are supportive of criminal activity, and are shallow, proud, or remorseless when confronted. This is different than the response given by a patient who committed an illegal act while in the midst of a manic episode or psychotic break.

ASPD provides some of the strongest evidence for the heritability of personality disorders. As children, antisocial patients are often innately aggressive, with higher activity and reactivity levels and lowered consolability. This may indicate an inborn tendency toward aggression and a higher-than-average need for excitement.

Conduct Disorder
"DDAVP"

Destruction of property
Deceitfulness
Aggression
Violates rules
People, property, and pets (animals) are affected

The first four letters constitute the major categories for conduct disorder. The specific acts are as follows:

"ID'S BRAT SWITCH"

Initiates fights
Destruction of property
Sexual activity has been forced on another person

Break & Enter
Runs away from home
Arson
Truant from school

Stolen items (confrontational and non-confrontational)
Weapon used in a fight
Intimidates others
Truth not told (lies)
Curfew ignored
Harms people and animals

* Recall that the **id** is the reservoir of instinctual drives, and lacks the capacity to delay these drives. Conduct Disorder can be understood as a child behaving as if he or she had an unrestrained id.

Avoidant Personality Disorder
"RIDICULE"

Restrained within relationships
Inhibited in interpersonal situations
Disapproval expected at work
Inadequate (view of self)
Criticism is expected in social
     situations
Unwilling to get involved
Longs for attachment to others
Embarrassment is the feared
     emotion

Essence of the Avoidant Personality
"A pervasive pattern of social inhibition, feelings of inadequacy and hypersensitivity to negative evaluation." (DSM-IV, 1994)

Ego Defenses
• Repression   • Inhibition   • Isolation   • Displacement   • Projection

Practice Points
• The Avoidant Personality Disorder (APD) shares considerable overlap with social phobia, generalized type
• A forerunner of APD was the "inadequate" personality
• Avoidant personalities desire close relationships, but are unduly sensitive to rejection; this is a key point in differentiating avoidant from schizoid personalities, as the latter are presumed not to want intimate relationships
• APD is often diagnosed in conjunction with other Axis I Disorders (usually anxiety and mood disorders) and other Axis II Disorders (usually schizoid and dependent personality disorders)
• Clark Kent, the mild-mannered reporter who turns into Superman (in a telephone booth), is an example of an avoidant personality
• MAOIs have been used in anxiety disorders, with phenelzine being the best studied of this group; tricyclic antidepressants, buspirone, SSRIs, and beta-blockers may also be useful
• A "need-fear dilemma" has been hypothesized to operate in APD

Differential Diagnosis

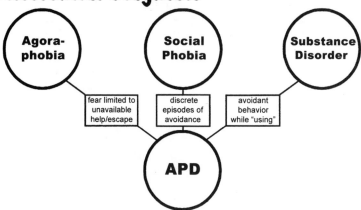

Avoidant Personality Themes
- Feelings of being defective
- Low tolerance for dysphoria
- Self-critical
- Exaggeration of risks
- Shyness
- Fear of rejection
- Hypersensitivity to criticism
- "Love at a distance"
- Seeks an automatic guarantee of acceptance
- Abruptly changes topic away from personal matters

Practice Points
- APD is one of the character structures most amenable to therapeutic intervention. If patients can endure the initial difficulties in therapeutic situations, they can integrate their growing tolerance for dysphoria into a more assertive approach to other relationships.
- Anxious and inhibited patients share some of the biological features of generalized anxiety disorder, particularly hyperarousal of the sympathetic nervous system. Tachycardia, pupillary dilation, and laryngeal tightness are common physical signs. Baseline levels of cortisol may also be abnormally high.
- Avoidant patients can be ideal group members and benefit considerably from this type of therapy
- A lifetime of avoiding relationships and social situations can leave patients lacking certain skills. Formal instruction may need to be arranged in areas such as assertiveness training, personal management, sexuality, and grooming.

Borderline Personality Disorder
"I RAISED A PAIN"

Identity disturbance

Relationships are unstable
Abandonment frantically
       avoided (whether
       real or imagined)
Impulsivity
Suicidal gestures (threats,
       self-mutilation, etc.)
Emptiness
Dissociative symptoms

Affective instability

Paranoid ideation (stress-related and transient)
Anger is poorly controlled
Idealization followed by devaluation
Negativistic (undermine themselves with self-defeating behavior)

Essence of the Borderline Personality
"A pervasive pattern of instability of interpersonal relationships, self-image, affects, and marked impulsivity." (DSM-IV, 1994)

Ego Defenses
- Splitting
- Dissociation
- Denial
- Distortion
- Projective Identification
- Projection
- Acting Out

Practice Points
- "Borderline" refers to the border between psychosis and neurosis; this disorder was initially called **pseudoneurotic schizophrenia**
- Borderline patients have impaired ego function, and are prone to decompensate under stress; they also have a poorly developed sense of identity (called **identity diffusion**)

Differential Diagnosis

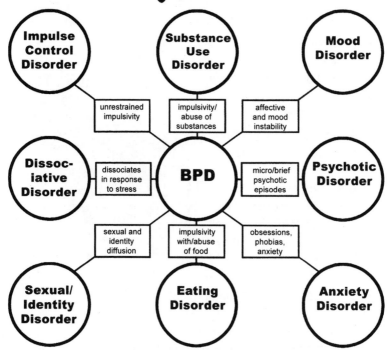

Borderline Personality Themes
- Chaotic childhood
- Parental neglect and abuse
- Self-damaging behavior
- Disrupted education
- Legal difficulties
- Substance abuse or dependence
- Sexual abuse; early onset of sexual activity; promiscuity
- Fears abandonment, maintains self-destructive relationships
- Failure to achieve potential or long-term goals
- Frequent suicidal ideation or gestures (burns, lacerations, etc.)
- Feels hurt by "all" past involvements

Practice Points
- Micropsychotic episodes are brief psychotic breaks that are usually self-limiting and last less than 24 hours
- Glenn Close played a classic borderline personality in *Fatal Attraction*; other good movie examples are *Single White Female*, *Malicious*, *The Crush*, and *Play Misty for Me*

Dependent Personality Disorder
"DARN HURT"

Disagreement is difficult to
    express
Advice – needs excessive input
Responsibility for major areas
    delegated to others
Nurturance – seeks excessive
    degree from others

Helpless when alone
Unrealistically preoccupied with
    being left to care for self
Relationships are desperately
    sought (when an estab-
    lished one ends)
Tasks – has difficultly initiating projects

Essence of the Dependent Personality

"A pervasive and excessive need to be taken care of that leads to submissive and clinging behavior and fears of separation." (DSM-IV, 1994)

Ego Defenses

- Idealization
- Inhibition
- Reaction Formation
- Somatization
- Regression
- Projective Identification

Practice Points

- A forerunner of this diagnosis was called the **passive-dependent personality**; it was seen as an immature reaction to military stress
- This disorder has both dependent dimensions (reliance of others, lack of autonomy, diminished self-confidence) and attachment dimensions (maintains closeness to others seen as more powerful)
- Dependent behavior itself is a feature of many other disorders (e.g. borderline and histrionic personalities, mood and anxiety disorders)

Differential Diagnosis

```
Agora-        Social          Mood
phobia        Phobia          Disorder
```

| fear limited to unavailable help/escape | discrete episodes of neediness | "clinging" behavior in depression |

DPD

Dependent Personality Themes
- Neediness
- Rarely lives alone
- Subordinates self
- Works below level of ability
- Continually seeks advice
- Volunteers for unpleasant tasks
- At risk for substance abuse, overmedication, abusive relationships
- Continual involvement in relationships; may endure a difficult one or quickly find another upon dissolution
- May have a "somatic orientation" by expressing their difficulties in terms of physical complaints

Practice Points
- Studies support experiences of both over and under-indulgence in the childhoods of dependent patients
- DPD contains concepts and criteria for both pathologic degrees of attachment and dependency behaviors
- Attachment behavior in DPD achieves and maintains closeness to a person who is seen as more capable; it is usually aimed at a specific person and increases a sense of security
- Dependency involves reliance on others, diminished self-confidence and a lack of autonomy; it is a diffuse process that involves seeking protection, help, and approval
- Advice, favors, and gratification of other needs are not a long-term benefit in dealing with dependent patients
- The neediness in DPD can manifest itself in substance abuse; alcohol and benzodiazepines in particular can provide a soothing, anxiety-dissolving substitute for attachment

Histrionic Personality Disorder
"I CRAVE SIN"

Inappropriate behavior – seductive or provocative

Center of attention
Relationships are seen as closer
than they really are
Appearance is most important
Vulnerable to others' suggestions
Emotional expression is
exaggerated

Shifting emotions, **S**hallow
Impressionistic manner of
speaking (lacks detail)
Novelty is craved

Essence of the Histrionic Personality
"A pervasive pattern of excessive emotionality and attention seeking." (DSM-IV, 1994)

Ego Defenses
• Repression   • Regression   • Dissociation
• Denial   • Sexualization

Practice Points
• Histrionic replaced the term hysterical starting with the DSM-III
• The concept of hysteria now encompasses several disorders: conversion disorder, somatoform disorder, dissociative disorder, phobias, and amnestic phenomena
• Histrionic patients relate the "weather" (emotions) instead of the "news" (facts); they also "miss the trees for the forest" in that their impressionistic cognitive style causes them to overlook details
• Psychoanalysis was developed by Freud to treat hysteria; insight-oriented psychotherapies remain a treatment of choice

Differential Diagnosis

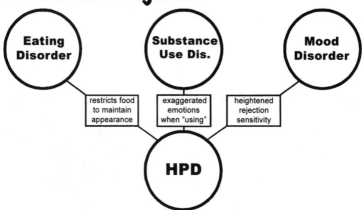

Histrionic Personality Themes
- Emotional instability
- Egocentricity/Vanity
- Suggestibility/Dependence
- Self-dramatization
- Exhibitionism
- Sexually provocative
- Fear of sexuality
- Overreaction/Immaturity

Practice Points
- Vivien Leigh portrayed excellent examples of this personality as Scarlett O'Hara in *Gone with the Wind*, and as Blanche DuBois in *A Streetcar Named Desire*
- The term hysteria is derived from the Greek word *hustera*, meaning uterus; descriptions of hysterical conditions date to antiquity when it was thought that the uterus could wander throughout the body causing symptoms at different sites; due to the ambiguity and possible pejorative connotation of the term hysteria, it no longer appears in diagnostic nomenclature
- In the left-brain/right-brain scheme, histrionic people are considered to be right-brain dominant; instead of answering questions with details, they give vivid but diffuse, global impressions
- Certain temperamental factors may predispose individuals to a histrionic personality style, such as: intensity, hypersensitivity, extroversion, and reward dependence
- Histrionic patients are considered to be fixated in a range between Freud's **oral** and **oedipal stages** of development

Narcissistic Personality Disorder
"A FAME GAME"

Admiration required in excessive
    amounts

Fantasizes about unlimited
    success, brilliance, etc.
Arrogant
Manipulative
Envious of others

Grandiose sense of importance
Associates with special people
Me first attitude
Empathy lacking for others

Essence of the Narcissistic Personality

"A pervasive pattern of grandiosity (in fantasy or behavior), need for admiration, and lack of empathy." (DSM-IV, 1994)

Ego Defenses

• Idealization and Devaluation   • Projection   • Identification

Practice Points

• This personality disorder is less thoroughly validated than other personality disorders; the ICD-10 (International Classification of Diseases published by the WHO) lacks a corresponding diagnosis
• Narcissus was a mythological figure who fell in love with his reflection in a pool; Freud brought this term into popular use
• Narcissistic patients commonly speak "at" instead of "to" others
• Narcissism is a normal developmental state (**primary narcissism**); in adults it is referred to as **secondary narcissism**, and can be a component of other conditions, especially ASPD
• Difficulties arise when patients' grandiosity is confronted with reality; patients can become hostile under such conditions and suffer a **narcissistic injury**, which can lead to a **narcissistic rage**

Differential Diagnosis

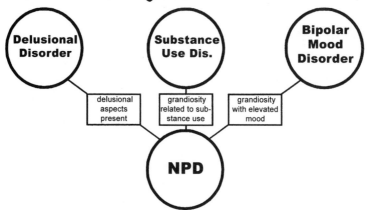

Narcissistic Personality Themes
- Condescending attitude
- Dwells on observable assets
- Hypersensitive to criticism
- Readily blames others
- Conspicuous lack of empathy
- Highly self-referential
- Difficulty maintaining a sense of self-esteem
- Many fantasies, few accomplishments

Practice Points
• **Kernberg** views narcissism as a pathological process involving a "psychic hunger" caused by indifferent parenting; some positive aspect of the child allows an escape from parental threats or spite; this "specialness" facilitates a sense of grandiosity that splits off from the real self, which contains envy, fear, and deprivation

• **Kohut** conceptualized narcissism not as a pathological deviation, but as an arrest in development; the seeds of NPD are sown when caretakers do not validate a child's responses; this empathic failure causes the child to develop an idealized image of the parents, rather than one based on real limits

• **Reich** recognized that patients protected themselves with character armor; he used the term "phallic-narcissist" to refer to individuals who were self-assured, arrogant, and protected themselves by attacking others first

• Narcissism is a component of several other personality disorders

• NPD can be difficult to validate due to the subjectivity of the criteria

Obsessive-Compulsive Personality

"LOW MIRTH"

Leisure activity is minimal
Organizational focus
Work and productivity
    predominate

Miserly spending habits
Inflexible around morals,
    values, etc.
Rigidity and stubbornness
Task completion impaired (by
    perfectionism)
Hoards items – cannot discard
    them

Essence of the Obsessive Compulsive Personality
"A pervasive pattern of preoccupation with orderliness, perfection-ism, and mental and interpersonal control, at the expense of open-ness, flexibility and efficiency." (DSM-IV, 1994)

Ego Defenses
• Undoing   • Reaction Formation   • Displacement
• Isolation of Affect, via • intellectualization
                    • moralization
                    • rationalization

Practice Points
• This personality disorder is not a premorbid condition for obsessive compulsive disorder; early descriptions did not differentiate between these conditions (hence the similarity in name); they are now regarded as two clearly different disorders
• Freud defined the **anal triad** as: parsimoniousness, orderliness and obstinacy (p.o.o.); Reich called OCPDs "living machines"
• Also referred to as **anankastic** (Greek for "forced") personalities

Differential Diagnosis

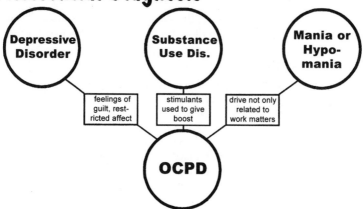

Obsessive-Compulsive Personality Themes

- Emotional constriction
- Indecisiveness
- Fixated on details
- Humorless; lacks spontaneity
- Cerebral rigidity and inflexibility
- Hoards money, objects, etc.
- Few leisure activities; can't relax
- Concerned with results, productivity and achievement
- Answers questions about emotions with thoughts – "It was my feeling that my boss was incompetent – I could have done the job in a much more efficient manner."

Practice Points

- Obsessive personalities relate the "news" (facts) instead of the "weather" (emotions); they also "miss the forest for the trees" because they are too focused on details to see the big picture
- The classic etiology of OCPD stems from difficulties arising during Freud's anal stage of psychosexual development (roughly 1 – 3y, corresponding to Erikson's autonomy vs. shame and doubt)
- There are no findings describing possible genetic links or physiologic abnormalities in OCPD; no less a proponent than Freud thought that obsessive individuals had a rectal hypersensitivity!
- OCPD appears to be more common in the oldest child in a family
- Cultural influences are etiologically significant; North American society in particular rewards independence, hard work, orderliness and punctuality (e.g. "Deal with it" and "Just do it")

OCD vs. OCPD

Despite the similarity in names, these are phenomenologically distinct conditions. Features that distinguish between the two are:

Feature	OCD	OCPD
Central Concept	Recurrent, intrusive thoughts and/or behaviors/mental acts	Enduring preoccupation with perfection, orderliness, and interpersonal control
Subjective Experience	Egodystonic; recognizes irrationality of mental events and behavior	Egosyntonic; doesn't seek help until relationships are affected or defenses break down
Impact on Daily Routine	Time consuming; interferes with ability to function	Defends traits and methods as being effective and justified by productivity
Mentation	Aware of forced nature of thoughts, recognize as a product of own mind; resists compulsions	Thoughts lack quality of intrusiveness; behavior occurs automatically, most processes remain unconscious
Manifestations	Often involve themes	Pervasive throughout
Anxiety	Marked; anxious dread	Not usually evident
Etiology	Growing evidence for genetic factors	Psychosocial influences predominate
Biological Features	Abnormal CT & PET scans; some structural abnormalities found	None consistently present
Treatment	Role of serotonin strongly implicated	Psychotherapy in various forms

OCD and OCPD were initially formulated as one disorder, hence the similarity in name. There are conflicting opinions about the degree to which OCPD may be present prior to the onset of OCD. OCD is associated with the other Cluster C personality disorders (dependent and avoidant) more frequently than it is with OCPD.

Rules of Order for the Malignant Obsessive-Compulsive Personality

• Being a Type A personality isn't good enough; strive for an A⁺.

• If in doubt, think, Think, THINK it out.

• The inkblot test has no time limit. After giving your response, clean up some of the mess.

• The more you do, and the faster you do it, the longer you live.

• If it's worth doing, it's worth over-doing, *right now* !

• The best reward for hard work is more work.

• Encourage others to do it by the book, **your** book.

• Perfection is the lowest acceptable standard.

• You can get all the rest you need when you're dead.

• The words **no**, **choice**, and **compromise** are not in your vocabulary.

• If you can't change the rules, change the game.

• There are others like you in every organization – find them!

• Burn the candle at both ends, and in the middle!

Paranoid Personality Disorder
"GET FACT"

Grudges held for long periods
Exploitation expected (without a sufficient basis)
Trustworthiness of others doubted

Fidelity of sexual partner questioned
Attacks on character are perceived
Confides in others rarely, if at all
Threatening meanings read into events

Essence of the Paranoid Personality
"A pervasive distrust and suspiciousness of others such that their motives are interpreted as malevolent." (DSM-IV, 1994)

Ego Defenses
- Projection
- Splitting
- Projective Identification
- Reaction Formation
- Denial

Practice Points
- PPD is not diagnosed if it occurs exclusively during the course of schizophrenia, a mood disorder with psychotic features, another psychotic disorder or is due to the direct physiological effects of a general medical condition
- Literally translated from Greek, paranoia means "a mind beside itself" and has historically been used to refer to a wide number of psychiatric conditions
- Paranoid personalities do not have ideas that are of delusional intensity; this is a key feature in distinguishing this personality disorder from paranoid schizophrenia and delusional disorder
- Paranoid patients are among the most likely to violent; to maintain rapport and avoid danger, don't challenge their ideas directly; take a "let's agree to disagree" approach in handling difficult situations

Differential Diagnosis

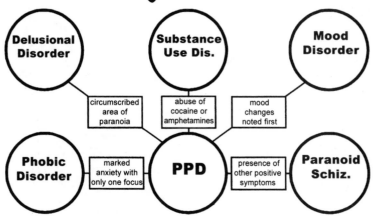

Paranoid Personality Themes

• Externalizes blame for difficulties – sees self as the continual target of abuse; constantly complains about poor treatment
• Repeated difficulty in dealing with authority figures
• Overestimates minor events – "Makes mountains out of molehills"
• Searches intensively to confirm suspicions to the exclusion of more reasonable conclusions – "Misses the forest for the trees"
• Cannot relax; displays little or no sense of humor
• Projects envy or even pathological jealousy – "They're out to get me because they want what I have"
• Critical of those who they see as weaker, needy, or defective
• Difficulty exuding warmth or talking about insecurities

Practice Points

• Antipsychotics have not yielded consistent results
• Brief psychotic episodes (minutes to hours) can occur, but since PPD is not a psychotic disorder, neuroleptics may be needed for only for short periods of time
• PPD can be a premorbid condition to an Axis I disorder
• Paranoid behavior can also be modeled – **folie à deux** is a disorder in which the delusion(s) of one person induce(s) another to believe the idea; though this disorder is usually seen in the context of a delusional or psychotic disorder (illustrating the power of environmental influences)
• Paranoid traits can be associated with developmental handicaps

Schizoid Personality Disorder

"SIR SAFE"

Solitary lifestyle
Indifferent to praise or criticism
Relationships of no interest

Sexual experiences not of interest
Activities not enjoyed
Friends lacking
Emotionally cold and detached

Essence of the Schizoid Personality

"A pervasive pattern of detachment from social relationships and a restricted range of expression of emotions in interpersonal settings." (DSM-IV, 1994)

Ego Defenses

- Schizoid Fantasy
- Introjection
- Intellectualization
- Idealization, then Devaluation
- Projection

Practice Points

- This personality disorder is not diagnosed if it occurs exclusively during the course of schizophrenia, a mood disorder with psychotic features, another psychotic disorder, or a pervasive developmental disorder, or is due to the direct physiological effects of a medical condition (DSM-IV, 1994)
- Schizoid Personality Disorder overlaps with the **negative symptoms** of schizophrenia (recall that negative symptoms are those removed or missing from the clinical picture)
- Schizoid Personality Disorder has a debatable genetic link to schizophrenia; the evidence is much stronger for schizotypal personalities
- In psychoanalytic and older psychiatric literature, the term "schizoid" referred to the DSM-IV concepts of schizoid, avoidant and/or schizotypal personalities; these diagnoses were introduced as separate disorders starting with the DSM-III

Differential Diagnosis

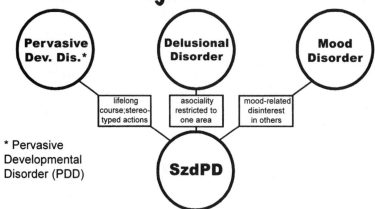

Pervasive Dev. Dis.*

Delusional Disorder

Mood Disorder

lifelong course; stereotyped actions

asociality restricted to one area

mood-related disinterest in others

* Pervasive Developmental Disorder (PDD)

SzdPD

Schizoid Personality Themes

- Prefers to do things alone
- Why bother? Who cares?
- Withdrawn, reclusive
- Works below potential
- Observer, not participant
- Lacks interests and hobbies
- Deficient motivation
- Goes "through the motions"
- May show considerable creativity
- Aloof, distant, cold
- Humorless
- Constricted emotions
- No apparent desire to pursue relationships

Practice Points

- Families of patients with schizoid personalities have a higher prevalence of schizophrenia, schizotypal, and avoidant personality disorder than the general population
- Analytic observations generally hold that men suffer more from disorders characterized by excessive isolation, and women more from disorders of excessive dependence (dependent personality disorder and depression)
- SzdPD appears to be a stable diagnosis over time
- Many of the world's great thinkers lived alone for the majority of their lives (e.g. Descartes, Newton, Locke, Pascal, Spinoza, Kant, Leibniz, Schopenhauer, Nietzsche, Kierkegaard, and Wittgenstein); even among notably creative individuals who did marry, there is an almost universal observation that their work was carried out in solitude

Schizotypal Personality Disorder
"UFO AIDER"

Unusual perceptions
Friendless except for family
Odd beliefs, thinking, and speech

Affect – inappropriate, constricted
Ideas of reference
Doubts others – suspicious
Eccentric – appearance/behavior
Reluctant in social situations,
      anxious

Essence of the Schizotypal Personality
"A pervasive pattern of social and interpersonal deficits marked by acute discomfort with, and reduced capacity for close relationships as well as by cognitive or perceptual distortions and eccentricities of behavior." (DSM-IV, 1994)

Ego Defenses
- Projection
- Splitting
- Distortion
- Schizoid Fantasy
- (Primitive) Idealization
- Denial

Practice Points
- This personality disorder is not diagnosed if it occurs exclusively during the course of schizophrenia, a mood disorder with psychotic features, another psychotic disorder, or a pervasive developmental disorder
- Schizotypal is an abbreviation of *schizophrenic genotype*; this personality disorder is considered a phenotypic variant of the schizophrenic genotype
- Schizotypal Personality Disorder overlaps with the **positive symptoms** of schizophrenia (positive symptoms are those added to the clinical picture – hallucinations, delusions, unusual behavior, a formal thought disorder, and inappropriate affect)
- Schizotypal personalities may decompensate under stress and develop **micropsychotic episodes** that last less than 24 hours

Differential Diagnosis

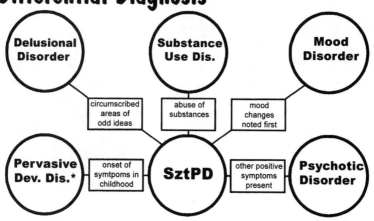

* Pervasive
Developmental
Disorder (PDD)

Schizotypal Personality Themes
- Clairvoyance
- Ideas of reference
- Suspiciousness
- Emotional reasoning

- Premonitions
- Alternative/fringe interests
- Existential concerns
- Magical thinking

Practice Points
- As with SzdPD, any disorder that is marked by eccentric behavior, isolation, and peculiarities of language needs to be differentiated from: autism, Asperger's disorder, expressive and mixed receptive-expressive disorders; language disorders are established by the primacy and severity of language difficulties in relation to other features
- Two conditions (no longer in the DSM) that overlap with SztPD are:
- **Latent Schizophrenia** – occasional behavioral peculiarities or thought disorders; progression to clear psychotic pathology does not occur; also known as **borderline** or **pseudoneurotic schizophrenia**
- **Simple Schizophrenia** – gradual, insidious loss of drive, interest, and initiative; vocational performance deteriorates and there is marked social withdrawal; hallucinations or delusions may be present but only for brief periods of time
- Physiologic findings in schizophrenia may also be abnormal in patients with SztPD (e.g. **saccades**, **auditory evoked potentials**)

Negativistic/Passive-Aggressive Personality Disorder
"NOT A COPER"

Negative reaction when asked to do something unpleasant
Overestimates task demands
Tardiness – deliberate slowness

Authority figures are ridiculed (without justification)

Criticism (constructive) is resented
Obstructs the efforts of others
Procrastinates
Evaluation of performance is unrealistically positive
Recall for obligations is faulty (forgets)

Essence of the Passive-Aggressive/Negativistic Personality
A pervasive pattern or resistance to external demands for adequate social and occupational performance (DSM-III-R, 1987)

Ego Defenses
• Passive-Aggressive Behavior
• Hypochondriasis
• Denial
• Rationalization

Practice Points
• The Passive-Aggressive Personality Disorder (**PAPD**) was included in the DSM-III-R, but excluded from the DSM-IV. It is now referred to as the **negativistic personality disorder (NegPD)** in Appendix B, "Criteria Sets and Axes Provided for Further Study." There were two main difficulties surrounding inclusion of PAPD as a separate diagnosis. First was the "situational reactivity" aspect, in that passive-aggressive behavior was seen only in certain circumstances, and was not as pervasive as the behavior in other personality disorders. Second, the disorder contained the single theme of resistance to external demands.

Golf Course of the Personality Disordered

Match the 10 DSM-IV personality disorders (and the passive-aggressive personality disorder) to the following activities:

Activity
1. Uses luminescent golf balls to play at night.
2. Spies on own ball to see who will steal it.
3. Assesses the energy field around ball before each shot.
4. Has fuchsia vanity plates on golf cart.
5. Improves lies to improve lies.
6. After a bad shot, makes the driver (1 wood) head the golf cart's new hood ornament.
7. Litters falsified score cards all over the course.
8. Forfeits game to help others search for their stray shots.
9. Carries golf bags for all other players in 95 degree heat.
10. Cleans everyone's clubs after each shot.
11. Develops explosive cough when others are putting.

Answers on p. 142

Airport Terminal of the Personality Disordered

Activity

1. Wears sunglasses and headphones to discourage conversation.
2. Conducts own luggage search after security clearance.
3. Refuses to get on any flight numbered with a 3 or a 7.
4. Announces own birthday on the P/A system during flight.
5. Hides contraband in little old lady's carry-on; retrieves after flight.
6. Punches check-in attendant when not allowed a free upgrade to first class.
7. Sews four stripes on jacket to impersonate the pilot.
8. Volunteers to help flight attendants serve meals.
9. Starts an in-flight daycare service in her row.
10. Arranges passengers numerically by aisle before boarding.
11. Boards early; has six pieces of carry-on luggage.

Answers on p. 142

Parking Lot of the Personality Disordered

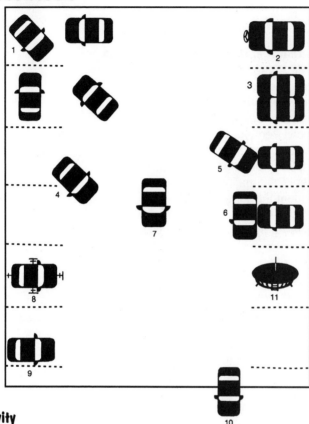

Activity

1. Cornered again!!
2. Largest car; prominent hood ornament.
3. Needs other cars to feel sheltered.
4. Angles car to take two spaces.
5. Rams into car of ex-lover.
6. Obstructs other cars.
7. Parks in center of lot for dramatic effect.
8. Perfect alignment in parking spot.
9. Hides in corner.
10. Can't tolerate closeness to other cars.
11. Intergalactic parking.

Answers on p. 142

Answers to Personality Disorder Quizzes

Golf Course of the Personality Disordered & Airport Terminal of the Personality Disordered

1. Schizoid Personality Disorder
2. Paranoid Personality Disorder
3. Schizotypal Personality Disorder
4. Histrionic Personality Disorder
5. Antisocial Personality Disorder
6. Borderline Personality Disorder
7. Narcissistic Personality Disorder
8. Avoidant Personality Disorder
9. Dependent Personality Disorder
10. Obsessive-Compulsive Personality Disorder
11. Passive-Aggressive Personality Disorder

Parking Lot of the Personality Disordered

1. Paranoid Personality Disorder
2. Narcissistic Personality Disorder
3. Dependent Personality Disorder
4. Passive-Aggressive Personality Disorder
5. Borderline Personality Disorder
6. Antisocial Personality Disorder
7. Histrionic Personality Disorder
8. Obsessive Personality Disorder
9. Avoidant Personality Disorder
10. Schizoid Personality Disorder
11. Schizotypal Personality Disorder

9. Cognitive Disorders

Delirium

Delirium is not an illness, but a syndrome involving a disturbance of consciousness. Cognitive functions are globally impaired, with an inability to focus or sustain attention, and often with abnormalities of perception. The onset is usually rapid with a fluctuating course.

Biological Features
• Common causes include CNS diseases, medical illnesses, and substance intoxication/withdrawal
• Some patients have psychiatric conditions that predispose them to develop delirium, but these illnesses are not the primary cause

Psychosocial Features
• Removal from familiar surroundings may hasten delirium

Mental Status Examination
• Disorientation with a fluctuating level of consciousness
• Hallucinations and illusions (in any sensory modality) can occur
• Language impairment (incoherence or rambling) is present
• Memory and general cognitive functions are grossly impaired
• The **Mini-Mental State Exam** (**MMSE**) is useful to gauge impairment and monitor progress

Biological Treatment
• The precipitating factor for the delirium should be identified and corrected as soon as possible (sepsis, drug interactions, etc.)
• Non-essential medications should be discontinued, and biochemical/hematologic abnormalities corrected
• Patients may need restraints to prevent accidental injuries
• Antipsychotic medication can diminish perceptual aberrations

Psychosocial Treatment
• Placement near nursing stations, illumination of rooms, and constant reorientation can be helpful during lucid moments
• Familiar faces, voices, and belongings are comforting

Prognosis
• Overall prognosis is very poor; the 3-month mortality is as high as 33%; the 1-year mortality is 50%; duration of delirium is a key factor

Delirium

"DELIRIUM"

Disoriented – time (most common) > place > person (least common)

Emotionally labile

Level of consciousness is impaired and fluctuates

Irrelevant stimuli distract the patient's attention

Rapid onset (hours to days)

Integration of perceptions is lost

Utterances – incoherent speech

Memory is impaired (especially immediate and recent recall)

Practice Points

• Perceptual disturbances, sleep-wake cycle abnormalities, and incoherent speech distinguish delirium from dementia

• Delirious patients frequently sleep poorly and experience a reversal of sleep patterns; a phenomenon known as **sundowning** may occur – this is an exacerbation of symptoms due to a less stimulating environment (less light, fewer sounds and people around, etc.)

• The majority of causes of delirium are due to medical conditions existing outside the central nervous system

• The hallucinations and delusions expressed in delirium are often of psychodynamic relevance; try and get as much detail as possible as it may be helpful after recovery

• Once treated effectively, delirium can remit quickly

• Anticholinergic medications are a common cause of delirium; unfortunately, many psychiatric medications are anticholinergic, particularly drugs used to treat extrapyramidal symptoms (known as **anticholinergic agents**) – if **anticholinergic toxicity** is suspected, physostigmine (a reversible inhibitor of acetylcholinesterase which crosses the blood-brain barrier) can be administered by IV as investigative and/or therapeutic agent; it is also used in TCA overdoses

• Many neurologic symptoms can be seen during delirium, e.g. incontinence, tremor, gait abnormalities, asterixis

• Acetylcholine is thought to be the major neurotransmitter affected; the reticular formation regulates consciousness

Dementia of the Alzheimer's Type

Dementia is a continual and irreversible decline in cognitive function (after the brain has matured), consisting of intellectual impairment with altered perception, mentation, and behavior. Dementia of the Alzheimer's Type (**DAT**) is the most common form, and involves impairment of memory, with at least one other cognitive deficit.

Biological Features
• Characteristic findings include plaques, tangles, astrocytic gliosis, and loss of neurons in a parietal-temporal lobe distribution
• Genetic factors are becoming better established; the dementia in Down's syndrome shares similar pathological findings
• A deficit of cholinergic transmission is hypothesized

Psychosocial Features
• 5% of patients over 65, and 25% of those over 85 have dementia
• Patients can develop a support network that covers their deficits
• A catastrophic reaction can result when patients become aware of their deficits in stressful situations
• **Sundowning** also occurs in dementia (see the *Delirium Section*)

Mental Status Examination
• Memory and general cognitive functions are the most impaired
• The MMSE is useful to gauge impairment and monitor progress

Biological Treatment
• Donepezil (Aricept®) is a reversible cholinesterase inhibitor which can improve symptoms in mild-to-moderate dementia
• Antidepressants, antipsychotics, and anxiolytics can be used for target symptoms; patients with dementia are very sensitive both to the direct and side effects of medication

Psychosocial Treatment
• Supportive treatment and education are beneficial; community organizations are helpful; optimizing the environment also helps

Prognosis
• Overall survival rate is about 8 years; a younger age of onset or family history often indicates a more rapid decline

Dementia of the Alzheimer's Type

"DEAR GRAMPA"

Decline in social or occupational functioning
Executive functioning declines
Apraxia – motor activities are impaired
Rule out – delirium, substance use, and general medical conditions

Gradual onset and continual decline
Relatives – runs in families
Aphasia – language impairment
Memory impairment
Personality changes can occur (disinhibition, exaggerated traits)
Agnosia – failure to recognize objects

Practice Points

• DAT and vascular causes account for over 75% of dementias; other common causes are neurodegenerative, infectious, traumatic, metabolic disorders, and dementia due to movement disorders
• Personality changes in DAT can become significant
• Psychotic symptoms (usually paranoid delusions) can occur
• An important psychiatric condition to exclude is depression; the poor cognitive performance is sometimes called **pseudodementia**
• Substance abuse, particularly with solvents, inhalants, or alcohol can cause dementia; heavy metal poisoning and organophosphate insecticides are important occupational causes of dementia
• **Benign senescent forgetfulness** involves trouble with word finding, but does not cause social or occupational impairment
• Medications commonly used to treat aggression in dementia are: propranolol, trazodone, buspirone, and antipsychotics
• The ability to focus and sustain attention is most impaired in delirium, it is less affected in dementia or depression
• In **mental retardation**, a normal level of intelligence does not develop, which is a key distinguishing feature from dementia

Neurologic Deficits Defined

• **Agnosia** is an inability to recognize objects despite intact sensory and intellectual abilities and language function. For example, patients can physically describe an object but not its function.

• **Agraphia** (or **dysgraphia**) is the inability to write (seen in someone who had acquired this skill). The ability to copy can still persist. The deficits with written language usually parallel those with speech.

• **Alexia** is the inability to read. **Dyslexia** is defined as an impairment in learning to read that leads to difficulties with spelling and the perception of the shapes of words and letters. Dyslexia is usually a developmental disorder, whereas alexia is usually acquired and involves a lesion in the occipital lobe.

• **Anomia** is a specific inability to name or label things even though they are familiar. This occurs whether the object to be named is shown or recalled from memory.

• **Aphasias** (also called **dysphasias**) are disturbances in the ability to express and comprehend language. The pathology is in the brain itself and not in the nerves or muscles involved in speech production. Aphasias are errors in word choice and grammar.

• **Apraxia** is an inability to perform learned movements as a result of disruption of areas controlling motor and language function. The potential to carry out and comprehend the movement remains intact. Apraxia often occurs with aphasia.

• **Dysarthria** is poorly articulated speech due to a dysfunction in the physical ability to produce sounds (e.g. mouth, tongue, lips, cranial nerves, throat). The speech of dysarthric patients is distorted and indistinct. In particular, consonant sounds are difficult to distinguish. Other abnormalities include added, deleted, or substituted sounds.

Medical vs. Psychiatric Speech Disturbances

Parameter	Medical	Psychiatric
• greater severity	+	−
• continuous duration	+	−
• abrupt onset	+	−
• older age of onset	+	−
• related language symptoms	+	−
• word finding difficulties	+	−
• awareness of difficulty (partial)	+	−
• loss of repetition, naming	+	−

10. Types of Therapy

Types of Therapy
"ABCDEFGHIJKLMN"

Addiction

Behavioral

Cognitive

Drug (medications – covered in Chapter 11, p. 171)

ECT – electroconvulsive therapy (covered in Chapter 11, p. 197)

Family Therapy

Group Therapy

Hospitalization (partial, day, or inpatient)

Insight-Oriented (psychoanalysis, psychodynamic psychotherapy)

Job (vocational rehabilitation)

Knowledge (patient and family education/psychoeducation)

Leisure (art therapy, music therapy, crafts groups, etc.)

Marital/couples therapy

Novel treatments (even psychoanalysis was a fad at one point)

Practice Points

• Psychotherapy can be defined as *the systematic application of a theoretical framework by a trained person in a professional relationship for the purpose of reducing or modifying symptoms, and to promote personal growth and development*

• Each form of therapy has its own indications, contraindications, side effects, and precautions (even inpatient hospitalization)

• Some treatments work well in combination (such as treating depression with supportive psychotherapy and antidepressants); others do not (such as concurrent individual insight-oriented psychotherapy and group therapy)

• Although there are hundreds of schools of psychotherapy, the broadest subdivision is between those based on **psychodynamic principles** and those based on **behavioral principles**

• There are many processes that operate to bring about change in therapy: interpretation, confrontation, clarification, elaboration, etc.

• In order to become a capable therapist, supervision is required

Addiction Treatment

General Principles
• Abstinence is the rule, very few can go back to controlled use
• Those motivated by close relationships are more successful
• Those who come voluntarily have the best prognosis
• Addiction is a complex phenomenon, with physiological, hereditary, congenital, developmental, psychological, familial, social, and cultural contributions

Detoxification
Done on an inpatient basis if the following factors are present:
• Severe intoxication or withdrawal symptoms
• Comorbid medical or psychiatric conditions
• Polysubstance use
• Failure of outpatient treatment or poor social supports

Assessment and Relapse Prevention
• Education about biological, social, psychological effects
• Diagnostic evaluation for pre-existing psychiatric conditions
• 12-step programs
• Medications can be used to:
> • lessen withdrawal symptoms (e.g. benzodiazepine taper)
> • prevent withdrawal entirely (e.g. methadone maintenance)
> • act as a deterrent for future use (e.g. disulfiram)
> • decrease craving (e.g. naltrexone, SSRIs)

Goals of Psychotherapy
• Focus on desire to be intoxicated
• Help patients acquire a higher tolerance for frustration and reduction of anxiety which can be accomplished through: relaxation training, assertiveness training, self control skills, etc.

Ongoing Treatment
• Urine testing – monitor abstinence
• Community supports: Alcoholics Anonymous (AA); Other 12-Step Programs; Al-Anon; Halfway Houses

Behavior Therapy

Behavior Therapy (BT) posits that all behavior is learned, and that undesirable behaviors can be replaced with ones that are more adaptive. BT is based on **learning theory**, which encompasses **classical conditioning** and **operant conditioning**. BT is applied without focusing on the cause (e.g. conflicts, childhood traumas) of maladaptive behaviors. Key names associated with BT are:
• **Joseph Wolpe**: Systematic Desensitization
• **H.J. Eysenck**: Learning Theory
• **B.F. Skinner**: Operant Conditioning

Classical Conditioning
A dog is taken to the veterinarian's office only for immunizations. When it is taken to the exam room, it sees the vet and is given a needle. Here, the needle becomes the unconditioned stimulus, and the whimpering is the unconditioned response. Eventually, the vet (the conditioned stimulus), without a needle will cause the dog to whimper (which has now become the conditioned response).

Operant Conditioning
Here, learning occurs because of an action that is reinforced by the environment (i.e. a monkey pressing a button to receive food).

Positive Reinforcement
A desirable consequence (a reward) is given shortly after a behavior, and increases the likelihood of that behavior continuing. An application of positive reinforcement is called a **token economy**. This is often used with seriously mentally ill patients, and involves rewarding adaptive behaviors with tokens that are exchanged for privileges or luxury items.

Negative Reinforcement
This occurs when the removal of an undesirable stimulus increases the behavior that preceded it. For example, children will stop talking when their teacher enters the room to prevent him from running his fingernails down the chalk board. The students do not get a "reward" for their obedience, instead they avoid the occurrence of an unpleasant event.

Relaxation Training

The most common method involves **progressive relaxation**, where patients concentrate on relaxing certain body areas in a given sequence. Often mental imagery and music are used to facilitate relaxation. At times, medications can be used as an adjunct.

Systematic Desensitization

Patients are first taught relaxation training. Then, they construct a hierarchy (graded list) of their fears, which usually involves about 10 stages. When in a relaxed state, patients then confront an imaginary sequence of anxiety-provoking situations. **Graded exposure** is similar to systematic desensitization but involves real situations.

Flooding

Patients are taught coping/relaxation techniques and then presented with a fear-provoking stimulus so that they gain mastery over their fears. **Implosion** involves imaginary confrontation.

Biofeedback

Bodily functions typically considered beyond conscious control (e.g. blood pressure, pulse rate) can be altered if feedback is supplied.

EMDR

Eye Movement Desensitization and Reprocessing (**EMDR**) involves inducing saccades (eye tracking movements) while someone is recalling a stressful event and then processing that image until the anxiety lessens.

Assertiveness Training/Social Skills Training

Enhancing self-esteem to assist in achieving goals.

Aversion Therapy

A noxious stimulus is given after a problem behavior is exhibited.

Principal Indications for BT

- Phobias, agoraphobia
- Sexual disorders
- Child behavioral problems
- Obsessions and compulsions
- Eating disorders
- Habit reduction/elimination
- Psychosomatic disorders (e.g. asthma, hypertension, headaches)
- Personality traits (Type A) or personality disorders (e.g. avoidant)

Cognitive Therapy

A **cognition** is a verbal or visual representation that comes into consciousness when one is confronted with a situation. Specifically, it is what one thinks *in* the situation and not *about* the situation.

This type of therapy was developed by **Aaron Beck** and is based on his observation that "an individual's affect and behavior are largely determined by the way in which he or she structures the world." Beck originally developed this approach for use in depressive disorders. He found that the style of thinking depressed patients exhibited reinforced a negative view of themselves, the world and their future (**the cognitive triad of depression**). Cognitive techniques are now available for many conditions, including personality disorders. Cognitive Therapy (**CT**) is short-term, structured and interactive. It has a "here and now" focus that is geared towards solving current problems. The assumptions on which CT is based are as follows:

Cognitions represent a synthesis of internal and external stimuli
↓
Individuals structure situations based on their cognitions
↓
Emotional and behavioral changes are caused by cognitions
↓
Cognitive therapy elicits an awareness of "cognitive distortions"
↓
Correction of these distortions leads to improved functioning

Basic Concepts

The genesis of a personality disorder, and some Axis I disorders, is biased information processing, called a **schema**. In essence, those with personality disorders think differently than those who aren't affected. The way that information is synthesized forms the type of disorder manifested (e.g. anxious people interpret the world as threatening, depressed people visualize hopelessness, etc.). Both genetic and environmental contributions predispose patients to interpret experiences in an altered way, which can initiate the disorder.

Basic Strategies

The process of CT involves an agreement between patient and therapist to explore and modify dysfunctional beliefs, called **collaborative empiricism**.

The next step involves the elucidation of certain themes that run through a patient's misperceptions. Like psychodynamic therapies, connections are made to previous experiences, so the development of the disorder can be understood. This is called **guided discovery**.

Patients keep a diary of their **negative thoughts** or **automatic assumptions**. This becomes the focus of the therapy session. These conclusions are constantly evaluated, subjected to scrutiny and reality testing, and then refined. The initial goal of CT is to have these automatic assumptions become more neutral or benign so that emotional and behavioral reactions are lessened.

Socratic questioning guides the patient and therapist to understand the problem and examine the consequences of maintaining maladaptive thoughts and behaviors. When patients see the illogical or false aspects of their beliefs, they are encouraged to alter them in a more adaptive and reasoned way. A **cognitive shift** occurs when patients gain a more realistic approach to processing information. This is facilitated by the exploration of maladaptive assumptions, testing their validity (**reality testing**), and altering them when alternative explanations or contradictory evidence are presented.

At the beginning of each session, the therapist sets the agenda, checks and assigns homework, and introduces new skills. Behavioral techniques are practical interventions designed to change maladaptive strategies, such as: scheduling activities, graded task assignments, rehearsal, self-reliance training, role playing, and diversion techniques.

Some Cognitive Distortions

Arbitrary Inference: drawing a specific conclusion without supporting evidence, or in the face of contradictory evidence

Selective Abstraction: seeing a situation in terms of a single detail and ignoring other possibilities

Overgeneralization: developing a "rule" after a small or isolated number of incidents and applying it broadly and to unrelated situations

Personalization/Excessive Responsibility/Self-Reference: attributing external events to one's self without evidence supporting the connection

Magnification/Minimization: seeing something as being much more or much less significant than it is in reality

Dichotomous Thinking: seeing experiences as being all good or all bad, e.g. something is either a great success or an utter failure

Catastrophizing: using a small setback as evidence of gross failure

Assuming temporal causality: seeing an connection between events which is artificial or coincidental

Principal Indications for CT
• Anxiety Disorders (OCD, specific phobia, social phobia, panic disorder, agoraphobia)
• Depression (non-bipolar, non-psychotic)
• Personality Disorders
• Eating Disorders

Family Therapy

While most types of psychotherapy focus on the patient as an individual, family therapy (**FT**) views the wider social context of an illness as crucial for both etiologic and treatment purposes. There are several different schools of FT, most of which adapt techniques from other forms of therapy (i.e. psychodynamic, group, and behavioral). One of the schools of FT which differs from other types of therapy is called the **general systems model**. Some of the tenets of this model are as follows:

• The marital relationship is a crucial factor in determining family functioning
• While a certain member is the "problem" (**identified patient**) everyone plays a role in establishing family patterns of interaction (e.g. scapegoat, rescuer, enabler, victim, persecutor, etc.)
• If the symptoms of the "identified patient" lessen, there is often a change in roles for all family members; at times the behavior of one member shields the problematic behavior of another

Bowen, a systems theorist, conceptualized the process of **triangulation**. Here, any two family members (generally the two who love each other the most, or who are in conflict the most) exclude others. When one of the outsiders becomes aligned with one of the original triangulators, conflict occurs, which is called the **hot triangle**. Stabilizing the hot triangle is usually the first task in FT.

Families have external boundaries and internal rules. In general, problems ensue when there are:
• Power imbalances (called **schisms** and **skews**)
• Malfunctioning hierarchical arrangements
• Unresolved family of origin issues (in the parents)
• Inability to adapt to changing family requirements and life cycle transitions

The major models of FT are:
• Structural
• Behavioral-Social Exchange
• Family Systems Therapy
• Psychoeducational
• Strategic
• Psychodynamic
• Experiential
• Crisis Intervention

Group Therapy

Group therapy is an effective form of treatment for many disorders. Virtually any type of individual therapy is possible in a group setting: supportive, cognitive-behavioral, interpersonal, analytically oriented, or educational.
Groups can be set up on an inpatient or outpatient basis, be open or closed to new members, be time-limited or open-ended, and have heterogeneous or homogeneous compositions.

Group therapy is an efficient treatment modality. In an era where the resources for therapy are under greater scrutiny, groups are gaining popularity and, in some cases, are an economic necessity.

While some patients do well in a group setting, others do not. It is important to keep in mind that within a given diagnosis, there is a range of functioning that should be considered when determining suitability for group therapy.

Group therapy is different from *The Bob Newhart Show* or the movie *Color of Night*. A group has an identified leader or therapist who uses strategic interventions and interactions between members to facilitate change. Unlike individual therapy, a group provides opportunities for immediate feedback from peers. Also, the group functions as a micro-society and is perhaps a more "normal" setting in which to view patients' interactions. This is valuable, because it allows the therapist and the patient to observe transference reactions to a wider variety of people.

Groups conducted for personality disorders are generally ongoing and open to new members. Ideally, a group has eight to ten members. Sessions are ninety minutes to two hours, once or twice per week. Socialization outside the group is discouraged, as is participation in concurrent therapy not involving (or not known to) the group therapist.

The theoretical basis for treating personality disorders in groups is usually psychodynamic. There are several powerful therapeutic factors operative in group therapy settings:

- Cohesion
- Altruism
- Universality
- Acceptance
- Socialization
- Catharsis
- Identification

- Validation by other group members
- Corrective emotional/familial experiences
- Learning from group members
- Internalization
- Instillation of hope
- Existential factors
- Imitation of other members

Interventions in group therapy are the same as in individual psychodynamic psychotherapy, though here they can be initiated by members as well as by therapist(s):

- **Confrontation** – calling attention to a trait that the person was previously unable to see; confrontations do not address motivation, they are made to point out the behavior; the group situation is particularly effective at bringing about a change in those confronted.
- **Clarification** – group members become adept at noticing repeating patterns in sessions; clarification brings particular actions into focus.
- **Interpretation** – interpretations are designed to make unconscious processes conscious, thereby revealing underlying motivations or conflicts; they help the patient attach a significance to events, feelings, behaviors, motivations, and conflicts.

Group psychotherapy provides an opportunity for interpretations to be made on a group-as-a-whole and an individual basis.

Peer interpretations can be particularly valuable, as members frequently have less difficulty learning about themselves with input from other group members. However, peer interpretations have a higher chance of being incorrect, poorly timed, or somehow skewed. In general, groups function more smoothly when members direct their attention to confrontation and clarification, leaving the more delicate matter of interpretation to the group leader.

Principal Indications for Group Therapy
See the *Insight-Oriented Psychotherapy* Section (p. 162).

Hospitalization

The process of inpatient admission is as follows:
1. The clinician determines there is the need for the person to be admitted to a hospital inpatient unit. This can be arranged on a voluntary basis (also known as "signing in," or being an "informal patient") or on an involuntary basis ("being certified," "being formed," or "being committed").

2. One or more of the following clinical situations is/are present, and require an intervention to be made:
• Imminent or serious risk of self-harm (suicidal ideation or attempt)
• Imminent or serious risk of harm to another person due to the presence of a mental illness
• Inability to care for one's welfare that will lead to imminent and serious impairment of the person
• Protection from social or environmental factors
• Failure of outpatient treatment
• Co-existing psychiatric and physical disorders
• Diagnostic uncertainty requiring evaluation
• The need for medical investigations
• Accelerated pharmacological management
• Specialized therapy only available or practical as an inpatient
• Any other situation requiring inpatient care

3. Administrative notification (e.g. Managed Care details)

4. The person is notified of this decision for admission as well as their status (voluntary or involuntary)

5. Consent is obtained to contact other people or agencies regarding the admission (e.g. family members, primary care provider, outpatient therapist); these contacts are made as soon as possible.

6. The clinician begins formulating a treatment plan, the goal of which is shared with the patient at the time of admission (if at all possible). This plan can be modified over the course of the admission due to:
• More clinical information becoming available
• Input from members of interdisciplinary teams
• Change in clinical status of the person
• Other factors

7. The person is taken to the admission area/inpatient unit where some or all of the following activities take place:
• The person's clothes and belongings are searched (for weapons, drugs, etc.)
• The person may be required to wear hospital garments
• Orientation to the ward and treatment team
• Physical examination is completed
• Bloodwork is taken
• Special tests are arranged if necessary (e.g. neuro-imaging, subspecialty consultation)

8. Further information may be obtained by members of the treatment team

Contraindications to Hospitalization
Countertherapeutic gratification of dependency needs; avoidance of social, legal, military or financial obligations (the **secondary gain** achieved by **malingering**)

Side Effects of Hospitalization
Regression; splitting of hospital staff; dependence on institutions; institutionalization; loss of pre-existing social, financial, or treatment arrangements

Insight-Oriented Psychotherapies

Psychoanalysis was pioneered by Sigmund Freud to treat patients with "hysterical" symptoms (which would currently be called a conversion disorder). While many of Freud's ideas and techniques are open to debate, there is little contention that he at least laid the groundwork for future generations of theorists. Several types of psychotherapy are based on psychoanalytic concepts:

- Ego Psychology
- Interpersonal Psychotherapy
- Object Relations
- Self Psychology

Initially, psychoanalytic therapies focused on the recovery of repressed conflicts. Bringing the intellectual and emotional elements of unconscious conflicts into awareness (consciousness) is called **abreaction**. In order to achieve this, Freud developed the technique of **free association**, where patients verbalize without censorship what ever comes to mind. Later efforts have focused on ego defenses and conflict between the id, ego, and superego.

These types of therapies are considered "insight oriented" in that patients are not explicitly told to alter their actions (as in behavior therapies) or change their thinking (as in cognitive therapies). In psychoanalytic approaches (often called **psychodynamic**), it is presumed that once conflicts are de-repressed and understood, actions and ideas will become altered.

Psychodymamic approaches are often described as either **expressive** or **supportive**. Expressive techniques are described in this section (p. 159 & 166 – clarification, confrontation, and interpretation) and are employed to uncover unconscious wishes, needs, and memories. Supportive approaches seek to maintain the status quo with advice giving, praise, reassurance, etc. In practice, both expressive and supportive approaches are used at appropriate times.

Principal Indications for Insight-Oriented Therapies
- Adjustment Disorders
- Anxiety Disorders
- Eating Disorders
- Gender Identity Disorders
- Impulse Control Disorders
- Mood Disorders (particularly Depression and Dysthymia)
- Personality Disorders (except Antisocial)
- Sexual Disorders
- Somatoform Disorders

Basic Psychodynamic Principles

There are some time-honored principles that form the basis of psychodynamic theory. As introduced earlier, the presence of the **unconscious** is an integral part of this theoretical perspective. Dreams and Freudian slips (**parapraxes**) are the two most common ways the unconscious is accessed. Symptoms and behaviors are visible extensions of unconscious processes that defend against repressed wishes and feelings.

Experiences in childhood are considered crucial in the formation of the adult personality. It is in these early years that the repetitive interactions with family members are of etiologic significance in personality disorders. Early patterns of relating to others persist into adult life; in a sense, the past is repeating itself. This was aptly put by William Wordsworth in that "the child is the father of the man."

Transference

In therapy, the process of transference involves a patient experiencing the therapist as a significant person from his or her (the patient's) past. Feelings, thoughts, and wishes that are **projected** onto the therapist stem from a previous significant relationship. In this way, the current therapeutic relationship is a repetition of the past. Properly handled, transference is fertile ground for learning in psychotherapy. Two key points characterize transference:

• The relationship is *re-enacted* in therapy, not just *remembered*; this becomes more obvious when one focuses on the **process** of the sessions with patients instead of only on the **content**
• The reaction to the therapist is inappropriate and anachronistic

Transference is not limited to therapy. It can be said that all relationships are a combination of the real relationship and transference reactions. Early attachments and internal representations of caregivers are so firmly held that they color future interactions. In this way, transference guides the relationships that people pursue. The unconscious influences behavior to a larger extent than is often appreciated. We seek out the type of relationship(s) with which we are already familiar, which is the principle of **psychic determinism**. However, people are not passive victims of their unconscious mental processes. There is room for choice and conscious intention in bringing about change, which is one of the goals in psychotherapy.

Countertransference

Harry Stack Sullivan said "we are all much more human than otherwise." Just as patients exhibit transference in their relationships with therapists, the converse also happens. Therapists are (usually) human beings who will, to some degree, unconsciously experience the patient as someone from the past. While many definitions of **countertransference** exist, Kernberg (1965) summed it up as "the therapist's total, conscious emotional reaction to the patient." Whereas a patient's transference is grounds for observation and interpretation, countertransference is not openly discussed in therapy. Constant internal scrutiny on the therapist's part is required to be aware of countertransference reactions. Though it can be tempting to act on such feelings, doing so only repeats the kind of relationships patients have experienced, rather than giving them the chance to learn. Instead, countertransference can be used diagnostically and therapeutically by allowing a firsthand awareness of how patients interact with others.

Countertransference

Transference

Resistance

At some point in treatment, almost every patient exhibits opposition to therapeutic efforts. Change is often accompanied by distress because there is an internal drive to preserve the psychic status quo. Whereas ego defenses are unconscious and inferred, resistance can be conscious, preconscious, or unconscious and is openly observed. It can take many forms: lateness or absence from sessions, prolonged silence, digression to irrelevant material, personal questions about the therapist, "forgetting" the content of past sessions, avoidance or failure to arrange payment, non-compliance, etc.

Resistance is a self-protective mechanism against experiencing strong emotions. As therapy progresses, these "unacceptable" feelings become less repressed and some type of resistance accompanies their expression. Just as countertransference is used therapeutically, resistance also provides important information. A psychodynamic approach provides an opportunity to discover what the resistance is concealing and what is being re-enacted in therapy. Though the term resistance suggests that it is an impediment, understanding resistance is a large part of psychotherapy.

By understanding the processes of transference, countertransference and resistance, the therapeutic relationship can be used to increase the awareness of how past relationships (**object relations**) affect current relationships, thus encouraging conscious decisions about changing maladaptive patterns of interpersonal behavior.

Therapeutic "Resistance"

Clarification

The therapist asks for more information from the patient to clarify his or her responses. In many situations when patients are distracted, upset, or not thinking clearly, they do not act in accordance with what is in their best interests. The process of clarifying maladaptive behaviors can lead to their diminution.

Confrontation

In confronting patients, you draw their attention to a particular behavior that is obstructing their progress (such as **resistance**). Patients may or may not be aware of the behavior you are pointing out.

Recall that **ego defenses** are unconscious mechanisms that protect against emotionally painful situations, such as blaming someone else for one's own forbidden wishes (**projection**) or transferring one's anger into socially acceptable outlets like contact sports (**sublimation**). In other situations, patients may be sabotaging the effectiveness of an interview for conscious reasons (i.e. malingering). In many cases, confrontations lead to the opening of new avenues of exploration.

Interpretation

The term interpretation has a variety of meanings. In the context of psychotherapy, it can be thought of as an hypothesis that the clinician suggests to the patient to explain discrepancies between observed behaviors and expressed thoughts or feelings (Campbell, 1996). Interpretations are used for a variety of functions in interviews:
• To assess the degree of insight a patient possesses
• As a means of overcoming resistance to the assessment
• To facilitate the sharing of thoughts and emotional experiences

There are three components to link together in an interpretation:
• The observable (or **manifest**) thought, emotion, or behavior
• The unconscious intent
• The reaction to the interviewer

Some therapists include a **trial interpretation** in initial interviews to assess a patient's suitability for longer-term treatment. Interpretations often follow clarification and/or confrontation.

Job (Vocational) Rehabilitation

Rehabilitation is often necessary for patients who have had extended absences from work for medical or psychiatric reasons. Vocational rehabilitation also helps seriously mentally ill patients develop skills that make them employable (e.g. punctuality, customer service). This type of training is often complimented by social skills training. The gains of employment go far beyond monetary rewards and include: less boredom, increased self-esteem, and improved social relationships. The principal types of vocational rehabilitation are:
• Clubs – resources are provided for patients to get training in interviews, preparing resumes, and completing applications
• Coaches – one-to-one onsite contact; the coach is familiar with the job and then helps train the newly employed
• Enclaves – entire departments (e.g. receiving, distribution) are turned over to a group of patients
• Transitional Employment – time-limited placement where job skills are acquired after the job begins (as opposed to prior); often an agency mediates and guarantees a certain number of employees
• Work Crews – patients travel to job sites with supervisors who are responsible for training, transportation, quality control, etc.

Regardless of the approach used, intensive support and positive expectations appear to be the best predictors of steady employment.

Knowledge (Psychoeducation)

Informed consent is a legal and ethical requirement to ensure patients understand their diagnosis, the risks and benefits of your recommended treatment, the risks and benefits of other treatments, and the risks and benefits of receiving no treatment.

The process by which patients become informed of their condition and treatment options is called **psychoeducation**. The other goals of psychoeducation are: to assist families in understanding their relative's illness, to assist with coping strategies, and to provide resources. The collaboration between patient, family, and professional is extremely important in improving the prognosis of many psychiatric conditions.

As an example, expressed emotion (EE – criticism, hostility, and over-involvement) is highly correlated with relapses in psychotic illnesses. The most significant method of lowering EE is informing the family about these factors.

In behavioral therapies, patients are told about the interventions that will be used and how they can help. Cognitive therapies also use psychoeducation as a core element. By explaining how cognitive therapy works (i.e. altering cognitive distortions towards a more rational, reasoned thinking style), therapists engage patients and make them collaborators in treatment.

Psychoeducation can be considered one of the key "social" avenues of treatment. Others include community resources, recommending books, social skills training, case management, etc.

Leisure Therapies

The use of the term "leisure" applied to these therapies is not meant to convey in any sense that they are less important contributions or are implemented just for the purposes of enjoyment. These types of treatments are also called **recreational therapies**.

There are four key types of leisure/recreational therapies:
- Art Therapy
- Music Therapy
- Dance/Movement Therapy
- Rehabilitation Counseling

Art therapy is particularly useful in treating patients who are dealing with traumatic issues. The creative outlet allows expression of unconscious material that may be too difficult or threatening to express by other means. The aim of art therapy is not to produce credible works, but to understand the relevance of what was drawn, sculpted, etc. to the patient's situation.

Music therapy can be viewed as an emotion-oriented therapy; the applications are impressively diverse (only a partial list is shown):
- Pain reduction
- Reducing depressive symptoms
- Traumatic brain injury
- Critical care settings
- Stress/anxiety reduction
- Palliative measures
- Dementia
- Bereavement

Dance therapy, crafts groups, and recreation are effective means of reducing the disability associated with physical and psychiatric illness.

"This is a therapy session. Lunch starts in twenty minutes."

Marital (Couples) Therapy

While being in a relationship is generally viewed as helpful and a good prognostic indicator, stresses do arise from day-to-day interactions even in the absence of mental illness. There is no single type of couples therapy, rather, there are many schools of thought based on other types of psychotherapies:

- Analytical
- Adlerian
- Behavioral
- Cognitive
- Reality-based
- Structural-strategic

Novel Treatments

Psychotherapy can be defined as "*treatment by communication: any form of treatment for mental illness, behavioral maladaptations, and /or problems assumed to be of an emotional nature, in which a trained person deliberately establishes a professional relationship with a patient for the purposes of removing, modifying, or retarding existing symptoms, of attenuating or reversing disturbed patterns of behavior, and of promoting positive personality growth.*" (Campbell, 1996). A far more cynical definition is as follows: *"an undefined technique applied to unspecified problems with unpredictable outcome; for this technique rigorous training is recommended."*

There is no single type of therapy which can claim to be superior to others. Innovations in, and combinations of, various forms of therapy occur continually and should be encouraged and given opportunities to demonstrate effectiveness.

11. Psychiatric Medications

Pharmacokinetics

Pharmacokinetics is the study of the distribution and metabolism of medications in biological systems. There are four main processes involved:

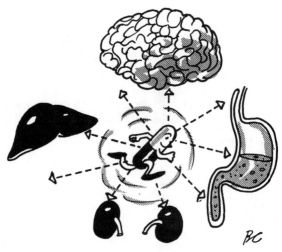

Absorption

Oral medications must dissolve and be absorbed through the gastrointestinal (GI) system; factors such as lipid solubility, pH, and GI motility affect absorption

Distribution

Medications can be carried freely in plasma or bound to plasma proteins (mainly albumin); in order to be effective for psychiatric conditions, they must cross the **blood-brain barrier**; the volume of distribution (V_d) is the body's available space for the drug to circulate (this is altered by age, gender, and medical illnesses)

Metabolism

Medications are biotransformed by four mechanisms: conjugation, hydrolysis, oxidation, and reduction; most psychiatric drugs are metabolized by the cytochrome P450 enzyme system

Excretion

Most psychiatric medications are lipophilic and are excreted via the urine and feces; however all body fluids contain some amount of medication (i.e. breast milk)

Pharmacodynamics

Pharmacodynamics is the study of how medications affect receptors (the site on a cell that initiates the effect of the drug). Medications can be **agonists** (fully stimulate receptors), **partial agonists** (reduced activation), or **antagonists**.

Psychiatric Neurotransmitters

"HANDS"

Histamine
• There are three known subtypes of receptors
• H_1 blockers are used to treat neuroleptic-induced parkinsonism and dystonia; also useful as hypnotics and anxiolytics
• Weight gain is associated with H_1 blockade

Acetylcholine
• There are two major types of receptors: muscarinic (5 subtypes) and nicotinic (1 subtype)
• Anticholinergic medications (antimuscarinic) are used to treat motor abnormalities (usually) caused by antipsychotic medication
• Blockade of cholinergic receptors causes: dry mouth, blurred vision, constipation, and urinary hesitancy/retention
• Breakdown of cholinergic transmission is thought to be a factor in various types of dementias

Norepinephrine
• Adrenergic receptors consist of $alpha_1$, $alpha_2$, and beta
• In general, psychiatric medications (antidepressants) increase norepinephrine levels (by either blocking re-uptake or catabolism)
• Improvement with mood is correlated with down-regulation of beta receptors, and accounts for the delay in improvement
• Alpha$_1$ blockade causes sedation and postural hypotension
• Beta blockade can reduce performance anxiety and tremor

Dopamine
• There are 5 types of dopaminergic receptors
• Three main dopaminergic tracts exist: nigrostriatial (movement affected); mesolimbic-mesocortical (psychiatric symptoms); and tuberinfundibular (endocrine function affected)
• Dopamine excess causes excessive movement, tics, and psychosis; depletion causes bradykinesia (as in Parkinson's disease)

Serotonin
• There are 7 subtypes of serotonergic receptors
• Overall, psychiatric medications increase levels of serotonin by blocking re-uptake or catabolism
• Serotonin depletion causes irritability and hunger
• Increased serotonin levels reduce anxiety and promote sleep

Neuroleptic/Antipsychotic Uses

"A BATCH O' SPICES"

Acute psychotic disorder

Bipolar Disorder – acute and prophylactic treatment
Aggressive behavior, **A**gitation
Tourette's syndrome
Chronic psychotic disorders
Hiccups

Obsessive-Compulsive Disorder

Schizophrenia prophylaxis
Parkinson's disease (psychotic episodes); **P**ruritus
Impulsivity
Cocaine withdrawal
Emesis (neuroleptics are potent anti-emetics)
Self-injurious behavior

Practice Points
• The above list includes uses which are approved and non-approved
• Flupenthixol in low doses may act as an antidepressant
• Neuroleptics are used in psychotic depression
• Typical neuroleptics cause blockade of the dopamine D_2 receptor (see p. 181 for clarification of the term atypical)
• Novel or atypical neuroleptics act on other dopamine receptor subtypes as well as other neurotransmitters (see p. 180 and 181)
• A neuroleptic withdrawal syndrome has been observed; it is more likely to occur with abrupt cessation from high doses
• Dopamine blockade in the mesolimbic area is correlated with reducing the positive symptoms of schizophrenia
• Dopamine blockade in the nigrostriatial tract causes the movement disorders of **extra-pyramidal symptoms (EPS)**
• Dopamine blockade in the tuberoinfundibular area causes endocrine side effects

Side Effects of Typical Neuroleptics

"HAPPENS WITH DOPAMINE"

Hepatic – obstructive or cholestatic jaundice
Allergic dermatitis
Prolactin levels increase – causing amenorrhea/galactorrhea
Photosensitivity – sunburn-like effects
EKG changes – prolonged PR and QT intervals; flattened T waves
Neuroleptic malignant syndrome (NMS)
Seizure threshold lowered

Weight gain
Impotence and **I**mpairment of other sexual functions
Tardive dyskinesia
Hematologic – leukopenia and agranulocytosis

Dystonic reactions
Orthostatic hypotension
Parkinsonism
Akinesia
Motor restlessness – akathisia
Insomnia
Newer/Novel antipsychotics cause fewer side effects
Eye changes – short-term and long-term effects°

Practice Points

° Chlorpromazine can cause pigmentation and granular deposits in the lens and cornea; thioridazine can cause irreversible pigmentation of the retina in high doses
• Low serum iron levels may predispose to akathisia; low calcium levels to EPS; temperature regulation can become impaired with neuroleptic use
• **Pisa syndrome** (leaning to one side) and **rabbit syndrome** (perioral tremor) are late complications of neuroleptic use
• Teratogenic effects are still being evaluated

Neuroleptic Malignant Syndrome
"COMMIT HALDOL"

Creatine phosphokinase (CK or CPK) elevation
Onset is related to use of neuroleptics (usually within 7 days)
Mutism
Myoglobinuria – can lead to acute renal failure
Incontinence
Tremor

Hot – temperature can become dangerously elevated
Autonomic dysfunction – BP, pulse, and respiratory rate changes
Leukocytosis
Dripping – diaphoresis and salivation
Obtunded – LOC ranges from confused to comatose
Liver function tests may be abnormal

Risk Factors Associated with NMS
"OH DARN"

Organic brain syndromes – mental retardation, dementia, etc.
High doses of neuroleptics

Depot or parenteral (IM) neuroleptics are more likely to cause NMS
Affective disorders – especially bipolar, or a mood disorder with
psychotic features
Rapid neuroleptization
Naive to antipsychotics

Practice Points
• Treatment of NMS consists of stopping the neuroleptic, supportive measures, and the possible use of dantrolene or bromocriptine
• NMS has a mortality rate of approximately 15%; early recognition is essential, as is investigating other diagnostic possibilities

Neuroleptic-Induced Tardive Dyskinesia
"CAN BET CLAIM"

Choreiform movements – rapid and jerky
Athetoid movements – slow and sinuous; snake-like
Neuroleptic exposure for at least 3 months

Bucco-lingual
Extremities   } sites to check
Trunk

Cognitive disorders – increase risk
Ladies – the incidence is higher in women
Age increases risk   } factors that
Interval – longer periods of use increases risk   increase the
Mood disorder – and other   risk of TD
              non-psychotic disorders

Practice Points
• Tardive dyskinesia (**TD**) is thought to be due to dopamine receptor supersensitivity resulting from prolonged blockade of receptor sites
• Any direct or indirect dopamine agonist can cause TD: some non-psychiatric medications are: **metoclopramide, promethazine, trimethobenzamide, thiethylperazine, trifluopromazine, levodopa, dilantin, antihistamines**, and **sympathomimetics**
• TD can occur without exposure to neuroleptics; it is seen in other disorders, but is not called *neuroleptic-induced* in these cases
• When the dose of neuroleptic medication is decreased, a **withdrawal dyskinesia** can result; similarly, increased doses of neuroleptics can temporarily mask TD
• TD can occasionally manifest as irregular breathing or swallowing
• There is no definite treatment for TD; management includes:
     • a rating scale (**AIMS**) for periodic examination (every 3–6 months)
     • reducing the dosage or switching to a novel antipsychotic once TD is detected; many medications have been reported to reduce TD (e.g. benzodiazepines, mood stabilizers)

Clozapine Side Effects
"WATCH PREVENTS LOSS"

Weight gain
Agranulocytosis
Temperature elevation (transient)
Collapse – when starting drug (avoid benzodiazepines)
Headaches

Pregnancy – fetal concentration higher than maternal blood levels
Rhinitis
Eosinophilia – may occur at beginning of treatment
Ventricular arrhythmia – torsade de pointes
Enuresis
NMS – has an altered presentation (i.e. fewer EPS)
T– wave inversion on EKG
Sexual – libido and erectile difficulties are the most common

Leukocytosis (tends to be transient)
OCD – symptoms may worsen
Seizures – risk is dose related
Sialorrhea – copious saliva; also gagging and trouble swallowing

Practice Points
• The trade name is Clozaril®
• Regular blood tests (WBC and differential) are required
• Agranulocytosis is a risk with any medication; always ask about sore throat, fever, sores around the mouth, and generalized weakness
• The risk of agranulocytosis is less than 2%; this must be monitored closely and the drug stopped immediately if it occurs
• Blood pressure and heart rate may increase
• Floppy infant syndrome and neonatal seizures have been reported
• Clozapine has less of an affinity for the D_2 receptor and more for the D_1 and D_4 receptors as well as acting at $5HT_2$ and $alpha_1$ sites
• Clozapine causes few incidents of **dystonia** or **parkinsonism**
• **Tardive dyskinesia** and **akathisia** occur infrequently

Olanzapine Side Effects

"PUT WHERE?"

Prolactin levels can increase (usually mild)
Uric acid levels can increase
Transaminase levels can increase

Weight gain
Headaches
Energy decrease (fatigue)
Rhinitis
Eosinophilia (transient)

Practice Points
• The trade name is Zyprexa®
• Drowsiness (somnolence), anticholinergic side-effects (dry mouth and dizziness) and weight gain are the side effects most commonly reported
• Weight gain appears to be most marked for patients who are underweight prior to beginning treatment
• Glucose dysregulation can occur with olanzapine in patients with and without pre-existing diabetes mellitus
• Don't confuse this medication with **olsalazine** (used to treat ulcerative colitis)
• Transaminase elevation is thought to be non-dose dependent and asymptomatic
• Routine liver enzyme monitoring is not necessary
• Olanzapine is useful for control of acute mania
• Agitation and aggression in dementia may respond favorably
• Self-injurious behavior (e.g. autism, mental retardation) may be lessened
• Can be used to augment SSRIs in the treatment of non-psychotic depression

Quetiapine Side Effects

"COLD SHAPE"

Cataracts – may develop (still being studied)
Orthostatic hypotension
Lipid levels may increase
Dyspepsia/dysphagia

Somnolence
Hypothyroidism (decrease in total T_4)
Anorexia
Palpitations
Edema (peripheral)

Practice Points
• The trade name is Seroquel®
• Quetiapine rarely causes EPS or prolactin elevation
• May be useful for controlling mood disorders
• May have a use in patients who are refractory to other antipsychotic medications

Novel/Atypical Antipsychotics
This list was accurate at the time of publication. Medications currently available are:
• Clozapine
• Olanzapine
• Quetiapine
• Risperidone

Medications in trials but not yet having approval are:
• Sertindole (released, then withdrawn to more fully investigate its possible link with arrythmias and sudden cardiac death)
• Ziprasidone
• Zotepine

Risperidone Side Effects

"HEPATIC"

Headaches
Ejaculatory disturbances (retrograde)
Paresthesias
Agitation, **A**nxiety
Tachycardia (due to hypotension)
Insomnia
Compulsions – may worsen if OCD is present

Practice Points
• The trade name is Risperdal®
• Akathisia and orthostatic hypotension are common side effects
• Of the novel/atypical antipsychotics, risperidone generally causes more EPS
• Prolactin elevation is frequent
• Causes less weight gain than other novel antipsychotics
• Useful in decreasing agitation/aggression in dementia

What Makes an Antipsychotic Novel or Atypical?
The atypical or novel antipsychotics are classified as **serotonin-dopamine antagonists (SDAs)**. Conventional or typical antipsychotics act at the dopamine D_2 receptor. In addition to this pharmacodynamic difference, Stahl (1999) summarizes the following points as being representative of a novel/atypical agent:
• Few extrapyramidal symptoms (EPS) compared to haloperidol
• EPS rarely develops
• Causes fewer cases of tardive dyskinesia
• Prolactin increases are milder than with haloperidol
• Prolactin levels rarely increase
• Better improvement in negative symptoms over placebo
• Better improvement in negative symptoms over haloperidol
• Effective for symptoms that are refractory to treatment by conventional antipsychotics

Antidepressant Uses

"BASIC BOD SUPPLIES"

Bipolar Depression – acute and prophylactic treatment
Agoraphobia
Smoking cessation
Impulsive behavior
Cataplexy reduction (temporary loss of muscle tone)

Bulimia
Obsessive-Compulsive Disorder
Dysthymic Disorder

Secondary depression in other psychiatric illnesses
Unipolar Depression – acute and prophylactic treatment
Panic Disorder, **P**osttraumatic Stress Disorder
Pain management
Ladies' disorders – Premenstrual Syndrome (PMS)
Insomnia
Enuresis
Sexual dysfunction – premature ejaculation

Practice Points
• The uses listed above cover all types of antidepressants
• Some uses have been demonstrated for only one or two medications (e.g. buproprion for smoking cessation)
• Although SSRIs principally inhibit serotonin reuptake, they do affect other neurotransmitter systems
• Antidepressants can induce manic episodes and rapid cycling in bipolar disorder; while any antidepressant can cause this, tricyclics and MAOIs are among the most likely to do so
• Doxepin can diminish peptic ulcer disease (histamine blockade)
• Therapeutic plasma levels for many tricyclics are available; up to a 50-fold variation can be seen among patients taking the same dose

Side Effects of TCAs

"NO BOWEL SOUNDS"

Nausea and vomiting
Obesity – usually only a moderate increase in weight

Blurred vision
Orthostatic hypotension
Widening of the QRS complex on the EKG
Ejaculatory disturbances (impaired sexual function)
Lethargy

Sinus tachycardia
Overdose is particularly dangerous due to cardiac toxicity
Urinary hesitancy
Narrow-angle glaucoma can be precipitated
Dry mucous membranes
Seizure threshold is lowered

Practice Points
• TCA often denotes tricyclic and tetracyclic antidepressants, collectively called **heterocyclic antidepressants (HCAs)**
• TCAs affect many neurotransmitter systems and can cause a diverse array of side effects
• TCAs are lethal in overdose; deaths have been reported at amounts only 3 times the daily therapeutic dose
• TCAs can have an antiarrhythmic effect
• Clomipramine is indicated for OCD; amoxapine has a neuroleptic action due to its dopamine blockade, and can cause any of the neuroleptic side effects (including **tardive dyskinesia**)
• TCAs can precipitate manic episodes or rapid cycling
• Plasma levels are available for some of the TCAs
• Vegetative symptoms (especially sleep and appetite) are often the first to normalize with TCAs (sometimes as soon as 7 days)
• The dosage needs to be increased or decreased slowly
• Warn patients to get up slowly when sitting or laying down

Side Effects of SSRIs

"THE NEW AGE"

Tremors

Headaches

Euphoria – induce manic episodes in bipolar disorder*

Nervousness – agitation, dizziness, restlessness, insomnia

Endocrine – **SIADH** and **galactorrhea** have been reported

Weight change (often loss; chronic use may cause weight gain)

Anorgasmia and other sexual side effects

Gastrointestinal upset

Excretions – sweating and rhinitis

Practice Points

* Selective Serotonin Reuptake Inhibitors (**SSRIs**) induce considerably fewer manic episodes than do TCAs

• SSRIs are first-line medications for treating depressive episodes (except for the melancholic type) and have many other uses

• SSRIs are safer in overdose (unless combined with other drugs)

• The starting dose for SSRIs is often the therapeutic dose

• When added to each other or other serotonergic drugs, SSRIs can cause a **serotonin syndrome**, a hypermetabolic state with: sweating, chills, nausea, vomiting, diarrhea, restlessness, myoclonus, insomnia, agitation, and possibly delirium; treatment involves stopping the drug, supportive measures, and possibly cyproheptadine

• Occasional neurologic side effects can be seen such as: akathisia, dystonias, and dyskinesias

• SSRIs can cause or worsen extrapyramidal side effects when combined with neuroleptics

• SSRIs may cause coronary vasoconstriction or slow the SA node

• SSRIs do have important differences (within the class)

• SSRIs have an impressive number of indications and uses

• SSRIs are best avoided in patients with sexual dysfunction, insomnia, and persistent somatic complaints

Practice Points on SSRIs

Citalopram/Celexa®
• Most selective of the SSRIs
• Fewest reports of drug interactions
• Some reports of carbohydrate craving
• Currently indicated for depression, but may have as broad a range of indications as the other SSRIs

Fluoxetine/Prozac®
• The long duration of action makes missed doses less of a worry
• Least likely to cause SSRI withdrawal syndrome
• Can be agitating – suggest avoiding in patients who seem anxious and who have trouble sleeping
• Will usually need a second agent to manage anxiety symptoms
• Most likely to cause akathisia

Fluvoxamine/Luvox®
• May have fewer side effects than most other SSRIs
• Least protein bound
• Usually causes sedation – give around bedtime

Paroxetine/Paxil®
• Paroxetine is the SSRI most likely to be sedating, making it more useful for insomnia and decreasing anxiety (useful in a mixed anxiety/depression disorder)
• No active metabolites
• Most likely to cause anticholinergic side effects
• Most likely to cause the SSRI withdrawal syndrome (see below)

Sertraline/Zoloft®
• May be useful in atypical depression
• Least effect on cytochrome P-450 enzymes

SSRI Withdrawal Syndrome

Neurological
• Myalgia, paresthesias, electric shock sensations

Psychological
• Anxiety, confusion, impulsivity, disorientation, slowed thinking

Somatic
• Fatigue, dizziness, sweating, chills, headache, incoordination, poor sleep, vivid dreams

Side Effects of Nefazodone
"HEAD BIDS"
Hypotension
Edema – in higher doses
Asthenia – weakness, fatigue
Dry mouth

Bradycardia
Insomnia
Dizziness
Somnolence – more common than insomnia

Practice Points
• Nefazodone (trade name Serzone®) has a dual action – it inhibits serotonin (5HT$_2$) receptors and is also a serotonin reuptake blocker

Side Effects of Venlafaxine
"DAD SINGS"
Diastolic BP increases – may remain elevated
Anorexia – may result in weight loss
Dry mouth

Sexual dysfunction – impotence, ejaculatory/orgasmic inhibition
Insomnia
Nervousness
Gastrointestinal – nausea & vomiting
Sweating

Practice Points
• Venlafaxine (trade name Effexor®) is a **serotonin-norepinephrine reuptake inhibitor** (**SNRI**); it may have a faster onset of action than other antidepressants

Side Effects of Buproprion
"A SPIN"
Agitation

Seizures – in higher doses
Psychosis – can exacerbate psychotic disorders
Insomnia; **I**rritability
Nausea

Practice Points
• Buproprion is a distinct antidepressant classified as a **selective dopamine reuptake inhibitor (SDRI)**
• Buproprion is available as Wellbutrin® and Zyban®
• Buproprion is active only in the CNS, it does not affect the heart, liver, kidneys, cause weight gain, or interfere with sexual functioning
• Bulimic patients appear to be at higher risk for seizures; the incidence of seizures increases with a total daily dose over 450 mg
• Buproprion may have a use in ADHD

Side Effects of Mirtazapine
"LOADS"
Lipid levels – cholesterol increases
Obesity – weight gain reported more often than weight loss
ALT increases (alanine aminotransferase – a liver enzyme)
Dry mouth
Sedation

Practice Points
• Mirtazapine is marketed as Remeron® – it is a **noradrenergic/specific serotonin antidepressant (NaSSA)**; it is unavailable in Canada
• No significant EKG changes have been reported; it is unlikely to be toxic in overdose (but can be a concern if it is part of a mixed overdose)

Side Effects of MAOIs
"PRIME SHOW"

Pyridoxine deficiency (vitamin B$_6$) – may need to take supplements
Renal – urinary hesitancy or retention
Insomnia
Myoclonus
Edema – usually seen around the ankles

Sexual – anorgasmia or impotence are the most common effects
Hypertensive crises – with the ingestion of tyramine
Orthostatic hypotension – the original use for MAOIs
Weight gain

Practice Points
• MAOIs are indicated for use in: major depression (especially with marked anxiety or atypical features), dysthymic disorder, social phobia, eating disorders, and anxiety disorders
• Tranylcypromine has an amphetamine-like action; tolerance has been reported with its use; it is a non-hydrazine MAOI with a more reversible inhibition of the MAO enzyme
• Phenelzine and isocarboxazid are hydrazine MAOIs; these drugs irreversibly inhibit MAO enzymes (there are A and B subtypes)
• Selegiline is a specific inhibitor of the MAO$_B$ enzyme subtype and is used for the treatment of Parkinson's disease
• Hepatotoxicity and psychosis are rare side effects of MAOIs
• Regeneration of the MAO enzyme takes up to 14 days
• MAOIs cause hypotension, but have fewer cardiovascular side effects than TCAs, especially on conduction and heart rate
• The MAOI diet is crucial to explain to patients (see page 189) – a consultation with a nutritionist may be helpful; there is a special MAOI diet for patients in hospital; this diet must be continued for at least 2 weeks after stopping an MAOI
• When MAOIs are stopped abruptly, a withdrawal syndrome may develop (agitation, nightmares, myoclonic jerks, palpitations, etc.)
• MAO enzyme activity (measured in platelets) should ideally be inhibited by 80% to yield a therapeutic result

Restrictions of MAOIs
"PASS BY ALL MEANS"

Pickled or smoked foods – especially herring

Aged cheeses – cause 80% of hypertensive crises

Soup stocks and soy sauce

Sausages – especially air-dried

Beans – fava bean in particular

Yeast supplements – e.g. Marmite

Alcohol — beer and wine (especially chianti)

Liver – chicken and beef (and human for that matter)

L-Aspartame – artificial sweetener (contains phenylalanine)

MAOIs – other drugs that have this action are SSRIs, clomipramine

Epinephrine – use with caution in allergic reactions

Anesthetics – may prolong sedation or hypotension

Narcotics – particularly demerol and dextromethorphan

Sympathomimetics – phenylephrine, phenylpropanolamine, pseudoephedrine, amphetamines, and ephedrine

Practice Points
• These restrictions apply to the traditional MAOIs – phenelzine, tranylcypromine, and isocarboxazid; a new category called **RIMA** (reversible inhibitors of monoamine oxidase A) have less severe dietary restrictions; moclobemide is the first agent in this class

• The ingredient of concern in foods is called **tyramine**; it acts as a pressor agent and can cause a **hypertensive crisis** (symptoms of a hypertensive crisis include: severe headache – feels like "head being ripped off," stiff neck, sweating, nausea, vomiting)

• Hypertensive crises can be treated with sodium nitroprusside or nitro paste; nifedipine has been used but drops BP precipitously

• Encourage patients to wear MedicAlert® bracelets or chains and to carry wallet-sized cards containing dietary restrictions

• Due to the short half-life, multiple daily dosing is required

Side Effects of Lithium
"THE MAGIC WAND"

Tremor

Hypothyroidism

EKG changes – flattened or inverted T waves

Muscle weakness

Acne

Gastrointestinal – nausea, vomiting, diarrhea

Increased weight

Cardiac arrhythmias – most common with pre-existing illness

White blood cell counts increase (leukocytosis)

Alopecia areata

Neurologic – memory impairment, slowed reaction times, etc.

Diabetes insipidus

Practice Points
• Lithium is indicated for the acute and prophylactic treatment of bipolar mood disorders
• Other uses include: major depressive disorder, schizoaffective disorder, schizophrenia (in conjunction with a neuroleptic), disorders where impulsivity is a prominent feature, and some general medical conditions (e.g. cluster headaches)
• Lithium is extremely dangerous when taken in an overdose, and can result in permanent brain damage; it is one of the few psychiatric drugs that can be removed by dialysis
• **Ebstein's anomaly** (of the tricuspid heart valve) is thought to be due to lithium administration in the first trimester of pregnancy
• Lithium is less efficacious for manic episodes with **mixed, dysphoric**, or **rapid cycling** features
• Levels are drawn 12 hours after the last dose and are also taken 5 days after dosage changes; levels for acute episodes are: 1.0 – 1.2 mEq/L; maintenance levels are between 0.60 – 1.0 mEq/L
• Lithium can be used to augment antidepressants and neuroleptics in the treatment of refractory conditions

Side Effects of Carbamazepine

"HEADS AND TAILS"

Hepatitis – hypersensitivity and cholestatic types
Eyes – diploplia
Aplastic anemia
Dermatologic – exfoliative dermatitis
Sedation

Agranulocytosis
Nausea and vomiting
Diarrhea

Teratogenic effects – i.e. craniofacial, spina bifida
Ataxia
Induction of hepatic metabolism
Leukopenia
Slows cardiac conduction

Practice Points
• Carbamazepine is indicated for the control of partial complex seizures (temporal lobe), grand mal (generalized tonic-clonic), and mixed seizure patterns
• Where **kindling** occurs, carbamazepine is thought to be particularly effective (kindling is defined as repeated subthreshold stimuli that eventually generates an action potential)
• Kindling may occur in the temporal lobes as part of the pathophysiology of mood disorders, hence the rationale for the use of anticonvulsants for these conditions
• Carbamazepine has many other medical uses including: trigeminal neuralgia, tabes dorsalis, migraine headaches, etc.
• Carbamazepine is marketed as Tegretol® in the USA and Canada
• Carbamazepine induces its own metabolism, which needs to be monitored (as well as liver function tests, blood cell counts, etc.)
• Carbamazepine also induces metabolism of other drugs metabolized by the cytochrome P-450 enzyme system

Side Effects of Valproate
"WATCH SANTA DROP"

Weight changes
Ammonia levels can increase
Teratogenic effects – neural tube defects, cleft lip, slowed growth
Cholecystitis
Hepatotoxicity – liver enzyme elevation

Sedation
Alopecia
Nausea & vomiting
Tremor
Ataxia

Dysarthria
Rashes
Oligomenorrhea and other menstrual changes
Pancreatitis

Practice Points

• Valproate is approved as an antiseizure medication for simple and complex absence seizures, and for multiple seizure types that include absence seizures
• It has a wide variety of other uses for medical illnesses
• In psychiatry, it is used for Bipolar Mood Disorders and seems to have a particular use in rapid cycling mood disorders and in **mixed states** (the coexistence of both manic and depressive symptoms)
• Other psychiatric uses include: reduction of aggression and augmentation of antidepressants and neuroleptics
• Hepatotoxicity can occur in children under age 2, especially if they have seizure disorders, metabolic disorders or mental retardation
• Valproate is thought to work by increasing levels of GABA
• Valproate can be combined with lithium and carbamazepine
• Valproate is marketed as Depakene® and Depakote® (divalproex sodium) in the USA, and as Epival® (divalproex sodium) in Canada

Side Effects of Gabapentin
"TAPER"

Tremor
Ataxia
Portly – increased appetite and weight gain
Elevates mood (in some cases)
Rebound symptoms – with abrupt discontinuation

Side Effects of Lamotrigine
"RASH"

Rash – in up to 25% of patients
Activating – may cause agitation
Spaced out – cognitive blunting
Hypersensitivity syndrome – causes a systemic reaction

Side Effects of L-Tryptophan
"GASSED"

GI upset
Anorexia
Sexual disinhibition
Somnolence
Euphoria
Diabetes – raises glucose levels

Practice Points

• Tryptophan has a variety of potential uses: adjunctive treatment of bipolar disorder (with a mood stabilizer and neuroleptic); potentiates antidepressants in treatment of depression and OCD; insomnia; may reduce aggression
• The **eosinophilia-myalgia syndrome** reported in years past with tryptophan was due to an impurity in the manufacture of the preparation, not due to tryptophan itself
• Use cautiously in patients with cataracts

Benzodiazepine Uses

"A SPAM PANIC"

Alcohol withdrawal

Sedation
Phobias
Akathisia
Mania

Panic disorder
Anxiety states
Neurologic problems – catatonia, dystonia
Insomnia
Convulsions

Practice Points
• Benzodiazepines are very effective anxiety-reducing agents and are used in many psychiatric conditions: insomnia, anxiety disorders, depression (alprazolam), mania (clonazepam), and akathisia
• Benzodiazepines have potent anti-seizure properties, and are indicated for use in status epilepticus, petit mal, and infantile seizures; the strongest anticonvulsant is clonazepam
• These medications are often used in medical procedures to enhance anaesthesia or provide additional sedation
• The strongest anxiolytics are lorazepam and diazepam
• Benzodiazepines bind to: a benzodiazepine receptor, the chloride channel, and GABA receptor
• Anterograde amnesia (memory difficulties taken after the pill) is the most common type of memory impairment
• Benzodiazepines reduce **extrapyramidal symptoms** after neuroleptic administration
• The key differences among benzodiazepines are their pharmacokinetic properties (onset of action, half-life, volume of distribution, metabolic pathways), not their efficacy or mode of action

Side Effects of Benzodiazepines

"ADDED TRAP"

Ataxia

Dizziness

Drowsiness

Erectile dysfunction – other sexual side effects reported

Disinhibition

Teratogenic – suspected to cause cleft palate

Respiratory conditions can worsen

Amnesia – anterograde memory difficulties

Paradoxical aggression can occur

Practice Points

• Due to the development of tolerance, these medications should be administered on a time-limited basis; dose and duration are the variables that determine whether tolerance develops

• High-potency benzodiazepines tend to cause more withdrawal problems

• These drugs are not usually lethal in overdose unless taken in combination with other medications or alcohol

• Benzodiazepine withdrawal can become life threatening; the symptoms are similar to alcohol and barbiturate withdrawal

• Rebound anxiety can occur with abrupt cessation, or if the dosing interval is longer than the half-life of the drug

• Combination with clozapine (a dibenzodiazepine neuroleptic) may cause severe complications; avoid use in sleep apnea

• Benzodiazepines increase total sleep time, but decrease stage 3 & 4 sleep and suppress REM sleep; this can lead to a rebound of REM sleep and insomnia when the medication is stopped

• Parenteral forms are available for diazepam (i.v.), lorazepam (i.m.), and midazolam (i.v.)

• Mild anticholinergic side effects can occur

• Flumazenil is a benzodiazepine antagonist and can be used in cases of overdose

Side Effects of Anticholinergics
"VECTORED"

Vision is blurred

Ejaculation is affected (delayed or retrograde)

Cognitive dysfunction (memory problems, etc.)

Tachycardia

Obstructions – bladder (retention) and bowel (constipation)

Respiration – asthma can worsen

Eye – narrow angle glaucoma can worsen

Dry – mouth and body (sweating decreased)

Practice Points
• Young men have the highest risk of dystonic reactions; pro and con factors for prophylactic anticholinergics are:

Pro

• Dystonic reactions are often painful and upsetting
• Reactions can occasionally be fatal (i.e. laryngospasm)
• Compliance with the neuroleptic may be increased

Con

• Avoid giving another medication until it is clearly needed
• Neuroleptics and anticholinergic agents (**ACAs**) are both anticholinergic; the combination can cause intoxication/toxicity
• Parenteral forms are available in the event of crisis situations

Effects of Cholinergic Stimulation
"SLUGGISH"

Salivation

Lacrimation

Urination

"SLUGGISH" mnemonic developed by: Karla Tinklenberg Jurvetson, M.D. Julie Tinklenberg, M.D.

GI upset (nausea, vomiting, belching, diarrhea, peptic ulcers)

Gasping – caution in asthma and COPD

Insomnia; **I**ctal events (rarely can cause seizures)

Sweating and flushing

Heart – bradycardia and other arrythmias

Electroconvulsive Therapy (ECT)

Indications – "CRAMPS"

Catatonia – in schizophrenia, mood disorders, medical conditions
Resistant depression
Acute suicide risk that cannot be managed otherwise
Mania that is unresponsive to pharmacologic management
Psychotic depression; Post-partum depression
Schizophrenia – early onset, and with a preponderance of positive symptoms that are unresponsive to medication

Side Effects – "A MATCH"

Anesthetic complications

Memory difficulties – anterograde more affected than retrograde
Arrhythmias
Tardive seizures – more common with preexisting conditions
Confusion
Headache – can be severe

Relative Contraindications – "FISH CAN"

Fractures of cervical spine
Intracranial pressure increases
Space-occupying lesions
Hypertension

Cardiac events – e.g. recent myocardial infarction
Anesthetic risks – e.g. malignant hyperthermia, severe arthritis
Neurologic events – e.g. evolving strokes, unexplained symptoms

12. Substance Use Disorders

Substance-Related Disorders

Substance-related disorders make an incredible impact on society, with up to 1 in 8 people affected. The DSM-IV defines conditions based on intoxication and withdrawal for each drug of abuse. Additionally, two use-related disorders are recognized, **substance abuse** and **substance dependence**.

Substance use can cause almost any psychiatric illness, with the substance-induced variant being indistinguishable from the naturally-occurring disorder. **Dual diagnosis** is a term used to denote the comorbidity of two or more psychiatric conditions. In practice, this often refers to a major clinical syndrome (e.g. schizophrenia) complicated by a substance-related disorder.

Substance use impedes a proper diagnostic assessment. As a result, a period of abstinence is necessary to determine if the etiology is substance related. Substance use also reduces the efficacy of treatment interventions, and obscures an evaluation of treatment response. In general, it is a poor prognostic indicator.

Drugs of Abuse

"COCAINE CHOPS"

Cocaine
Opioids
Cannabis
Amphetamines
Inhalants and Solvents
Nicotine
Ethanol and non-beverage alcohol

Caffeine
Hallucinogens
Other
PCP – phencyclidine
Sedative-hypnotics

Substance Abuse
"HELP"

Hazardous circumstances do not deter substance use
Evasion of obligations due to substance use
Legal difficulties caused by use of substances
Problems (social and interpersonal) develop due to use

Substance Dependence
"ROLAID PUPILS"

Relief of withdrawal symptoms occurs with substance use
      (withdrawal criterion #2)
Occupational/social/recreational activities are given up or reduced
Larger amounts are taken than originally intended
Awareness of problems related to substance use
Increased amounts are needed to achieve the same effect
      (tolerance criterion #1)
Diminished effect with use of the same amount of the substance
      (tolerance criterion #2)

Persistent desire to cut down or control use
Unsuccessful efforts to cut down or control use
Personal problems (social and interpersonal) due to use
Investment of time in substance-related activity is considerable
Longer duration of use than initially intended
Symptoms of withdrawal occur (withdrawal criterion #1)

Practice Points
• The signs and symptoms of dependence or abuse must be present within the same 12-month period
• Dependence is a more serious condition than abuse; if the criteria for substance dependence have been met, substance abuse is not diagnosed
• Almost any psychiatric illness can be caused or mimicked by substance use – ask all patients about their use of substances

Alcohol, Sedative-Hypnotic & Anxiolytic Intoxication

"I'M SINGING"

Ingestion must have occurred
Maladaptive behavior is related to ingestion

Speech is slurred
Incoordination
Nystagmus
Gait is unsteady
Inattention and memory deficits
Numb – pain threshold increases
General medical conditions excluded (e.g. diabetes)

Amphetamine/Cocaine Intoxication

"DARN BAD SPIN"
Dilated pupils
Arrythmias
Respiratory depression
Nausea or vomiting

Blood pressure changes – may increase or decrease
Anorexia – evidence of weight loss
Drive (drivenness) changes – psychomotor agitation or retardation

Sweating – perspiration or chills
Pulse changes – either tachycardia or bradycardia
Ingestion
Neurologic abnormalities – confusion, seizures, dyskinesias, etc.

Caffeine Intoxication

"I FARM GRENADES"

Insomnia

Flushed face
Arrhythmia
Rambling – thought and speech
Muscle twitching

GI (gastrointestinal) disturbances
Restlessness
Excitement
Nervousness
Agitation
Diuresis
Energy level increases
Several cups of coffee (250mg or more of caffeine)

Cannabis Intoxication

"MATCH"

Mouth is dry
Appetite increases – "the munchies"
Tachycardia
Conjunctival injection
Heightened sensitivity to stimuli

There is no recognized withdrawal syndrome, though psychological dependence can occur.

Hallucinogen Intoxication
"VISIT THE PAST"

Vision is blurred
Incoordination
Synesthesias (a blending of sensory perceptions)
Illusions
Tremors

Thought content changes – ideas of reference, paranoia, etc.
Hallucinations
Euphoria

Pupillary dilation, **P**alpitations
Altered perception – depersonalization, derealization, etc.
Sweating
Tachycardia

There is no recognized withdrawal syndrome, though psychological dependence can occur.

Opioid Intoxication
"JADED PAST"

Judgment is impaired
Apathy (after initial euphoria)
Dysphoria
Eye changes – constriction
Drowsiness

Psychomotor changes
Attention is impaired
Speech is slurred
Triad – of coma, pinpoint pupils, and respiratory depression is consistent with an opioid overdose

Inhalant Intoxication
"GASOLINE DART"
Gait is unsteady
Aggressiveness or assaultiveness
Speech is slurred
Ocular changes – blurred vision or diploplia
Lethargy
Incoordination
Nystagmus
Euphoria

Dizziness
Apathy
Reflexes are depressed
Tremor

There is no recognized withdrawal syndrome, though psychological dependence can occur.

Phencyclidine Intoxication
"DARN PHDs"
Disorientation
Ataxia
Rigidity
Nystagmus (horizontal or vertical)

Pain threshold decreased
Hallucinations, **H**yperacusis
Dysarthria
Seizures

There is no recognized withdrawal syndrome, though psychological dependence can occur.

Alcohol, Sedative-Hypnotic & Anxiolytic Withdrawal

"PINT OF ASA"

Perceptual disturbances – hallucinations or illusions

Insomnia, **I**rritability

Nausea, vomiting

Tremor – usually seen in the hands

Onset is from hours to 3 days after last consumption

Flushing of the face seen

Autonomic hyperactivity – heart rate, blood pressure, temperature

Seizures – grand mal (tonic-clonic)

Agitation

Practice Points

- Alcohol withdrawal is more likely to occur with heavy, prolonged consumption in the presence of malnourishment and coexisting physical ailments
- Patients with seizures that persist beyond 48 hours should be investigated for other conditions
- Administer thiamine (vitamin B_1) prior to giving food or glucose; Wernicke-Korsakoff syndrome (ataxia, confusion, ophthalmoplegia) can be precipitated by giving glucose first
- Long-acting benzodiazepines are the mainstay of treatment (chlorazepate, chlordiazepoxide, diazepam); multivitamins and magnesium are often added
- In patients with severe liver disease, use lorazepam, oxazepam, or temazepam (LOT) to avoid accumulation of active metabolites
- **Delirium tremens** (**DTs** – alcohol withdrawal delirium) is a complication of alcohol withdrawal; the onset is 1 to 3 days after cessation of drinking; mortality rates can be as high as 20%
- Patients with alcohol use disorders commonly fall or get into physical fights – remember to consider a subdural hematoma
- Withdrawal seizures do not generally require prophylaxis or continuation of treatment after the withdrawal has passed

Amphetamine/Cocaine Withdrawal
"SPACED"

Sleep problems – insomnia or hypersomnia
Psychomotor changes – agitation or retardation
Appetite increases
Crusty mood – dysphoria
Energy level decreases – fatigue
Dreams – unpleasant and vivid

Caffeine Withdrawal
"MAD FISH"

Muscle pain and stiffness
Anxiety
Depression

Fatigue or drowsiness
Irritability
Stomach upset (nausea or vomiting)
Headache

Nicotine Withdrawal
"BIC TRIAD"

Bradycardia
Irritability
Concentration is poor

Tense, anxious
Restless
Insomnia
Appetite increases
Dysphoric mood

Opioid Withdrawal

"A MANY PAIN DEAL"

Antagonist precipitates withdrawal *

Mood is dysphoric
Aches in muscles and bones
Nausea, vomiting
Yawning

Piloerection – "gooseflesh" (the origin of the term "cold turkey")
Agonist removes withdrawal symptoms
Insomnia
Not life threatening

Diarrhea
Elevated temperature
Abdominal cramps
Lacrimation and rhinorrhea

Practice Points
* Opioid antagonists (naloxone, naltrexone) can block the euphoric effects that accompany the use of morphine, heroin, demerol, etc.
• Avoid using demerol (meperidine) with MAOIs
• Constipation and miosis don't diminish with tolerance
• Withdrawal from short-acting opioids can occur as soon as 6 hours, and up to 3 days for longer-acting opioids
• Any opioid can reverse withdrawal symptoms
• In practice, methadone and LAMM are used to treat withdrawal symptoms – they are synthetic opioids that can be taken orally and have a long duration of action with a minimal degree of euphoria
• **Methadone maintenance programs** defer the withdrawal until patients are better prepared; these programs also reduce the use of needles, a major factor in the spread of HIV, hepatitis B, and other intravenously transmitted infections

13. Treatment Planning

Psychiatric Differential Diagnosis

"OF SIG'S SPACED CAMPS"

Other Conditions that may be a focus of clinical attention
Factitious Disorders

Sleep Disorders
Impulse-Control Disorders
Gender Identity Disorders
Sexual Disorders

Somatoform Disorders
Personality Disorders
Anxiety Disorders
Cognitive Disorders
Eating Disorders
Dissociative Disorders

Conversion Disorders
Adjustment Disorders
Mood Disorders
Psychotic Disorders
Substance-Related Disorders

This mnemonic lists all of the DSM-IV categories for psychiatric conditions. This is useful in constructing a **differential diagnosis**, which is a list of alternate or possible diagnoses that patients may have. It is important to keep a range of diagnostic possibilities in mind as new information becomes available.

Psychiatric Admission Orders

"A SMART LIST TO RECALL"

Attending Physician/Service

Status (voluntary or involuntary; legal situation regarding admission)
Monitoring (observation level, vital signs, etc.)
Attire (own clothes, hospital pajamas, etc.)
Restraints (chemical, physical, locked room or ward, etc.)
Three Squares (diet – regular, MAOI diet, food allergies, etc.)

Levels (for applicable medications – lithium, carbamazepine, etc.)
Investigations (blood counts, electrolytes, relevant organ testing)
Supplemental information (old chart, signed consents for records)
Tests (if indicated, e.g. EKG, EEG, CXR, CT, or MRI scans, etc.)

Therapeutic medications (antipsychotics, antidepressants, etc.)
Other medications (non-psychiatric medications)

Referrals (other medical specialties, psychological testing, etc.)
Evening – hs (bedtime) sedation (commonly requested)
Calming medications (anxiolytics are commonly requested)
Analgesics (commonly requested)
Laxatives (commonly requested)
Letters (for work, school, etc. if needed to account for absence)

Practice Points
- Check for MedicAlert® bracelets and chains
- Ask about food and drug allergies
- Consider leaving an order for anticholinergic medication to treat dystonic reactions when using conventional antipsychotics (see p. 196)
- Warn patients about expectable side effects to their medications
- Search patients' clothes and belongings for medications, weapons, electrical appliances, lighters, matches, rope, razor blades, etc.

Biopsychosocial Management Plan

> **Assessment in a clinic or outpatient setting**
> • Is admission to hospital necessary?
> • Does the situation warrant an involuntary admission?

Investigations

Biological
- Admission physical exam
- Diagnostic tests:
    Routine: *hematologic and clinical chemistry admission/screening bloodwork*
    Toxicology: *serum medication levels; urine screen for substances of abuse; special assays*
- Diagnostic investigations: CXR, EKG
- Neuroimaging: CT, MRI scans
- EEG
- Consultations with other medical specialties
- Special tests:
    hypothalamic/pituitary/adrenal axis testing (DST, TRH stimulation test, GH response) sleep studies other

Social
- Collateral history:
    *friends and family members
    primary care physician
    community psychiatrist
    other clinics, programs or hospitals*
- Activities of Daily Living **(ADL)** and Instrumental Activities of Daily Living **(IADL)** assessment
- Referral to members of multidisciplinary team
    social worker; occupational therapist; physiotherapist; dietician; clergy; nurse clinician

Psycho-logical
- Personality and Intelligence tests
- Cognitive screening tests (e.g. Mini-Mental State Exam, clock drawing, etc.)
- Neuropsychological test batteries
- Structured interviews/diagnostic testing

Treatment — Short Term

Biological
- Psychopharmacology
  - *antidepressants*
  - *antiparkinsonian agents*
  - *antipsychotics*
  - *anxiolytics*
  - *mood stabilizers*
  - *psychostimulants*
  - *sedative/hypnotics*
  - *other*
- ECT
- Other psychiatric treatments
- Somatic illnesses
  - *medications, physical treatments*
- Detoxification from medications or substances
- Environmental
  - *level of observation*
  - *passes*
  - *attire (pajamas or street clothes)*
  - *seclusion rooms; mechanical restraints*
  - *objects to assist with reorientation*

Social
- Social services
  - *assistance with housing, finances, etc.*
- Education and focus/support groups
- Occupational Therapy
- Family meetings
- Administrative
  - *voluntary/involuntary status*
  - *rights/legal advice*
  - *duty to warn/duty to protect others*
  - *treatment contracts*
  - *informing work/school of absence*
  - *substitute consent if deemed incapable*

Psycho-logical
- Advice/Reality Therapy
- Behavior Therapy/Modification
- Cognitive Therapy
- Group Therapy
- Milieu Therapy
- Recreation Therapy
- Stress Management
- Other therapies with a shorter-term focus

Treatment — Longer Term

Biological
- Reduction/optimization of dosage
- Depot antipsychotic medications
- Monitoring vulnerable organ systems
- Serum level monitoring
- Adjunct/augmentation/combination treatments
- Factors reducing the efficacy of medication
    - *nicotine*
    - *caffeine*
    - *liver enzyme inducers*
    - *others*
- Health teaching and lifestyle changes

Social
- Vocational rehabilitation
- Religious guidance
- Community supports and organizations
- Discharge planning
    - *transfer to another facility*
    - *housing options*
    - *case manager*
- Liaison with general practitioner

Psycho-logical
- Psychotherapy
  continuation of inpatient therapy
  arrange outpatient treatment
- Match various types of therapies to needs and attainable goals for the patient

The Biopsychosocial Grid

	Biological	Psychological	Social
Investigations			
Short-Term Treatment			
Longer-Term Treatment			

14. Consultation- Liaison Psychiatry

What is Consultation-Liaison Psychiatry?

Consultation-Liaison (C-L) refers to the branch or subspecialty of psychiatry that focuses on the interface between psychological (mental) and somatic (medical) illnesses. The main function of C-L psychiatry is to provide clinical services that link mental health professionals to those in other medical specialties (as illustrated below), on both an inpatient and outpatient basis. C-L psychiatry also has education and research components. C-L psychiatry can be conceptualized as bridging the gap between illnesses which are entirely physical in nature and those considered to have entirely psychological causes.

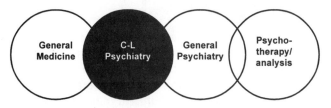

Consultation Psychiatry

Although the term **C-L** is usually globally applied to the activities described above, **consultation** and **liaison** in practice encompass separate functions. **Consultation** refers to the provision of clinical services for a patient at the request of the primary (non-psychiatric) physician. The consultation involves an interview, followed by the development and implementation of a treatment plan. The aim is to answer the clinical question(s) posed by the referring physician, and to assist in the management of the central problem and related issues. The consultation model requires the consultee to initiate the process. Requests are made once problems have developed and have been recognized. In this way, the consultations focus on **secondary prevention** (limiting the progression of symptoms after they have developed) and **tertiary prevention** (rehabilitating patients to prevent the recurrence of symptoms). There is no structured teaching of psychiatric principles, though clinical points germane to the particular case may be emphasized. Consultation services meet the basic clinical needs of referring sources.

Liaison Psychiatry

Liaison refers to activities that promote an awareness of psychiatric and psychosocial issues in patients' care. These educational contacts can be either formal (e.g. structured teaching rounds) or informal, and are carried out to:
• Increase the attention paid to the psychosocial aspects of a patient's care and to practice **primary prevention** strategies (preventing the development of psychological symptoms)
• Educate medical/surgical colleagues about the psychological effects of being ill, and how this affects recovery
• Impart basic psychosocial knowledge and help foster the ability of other physicians in detection and triage techniques

Receiving the Referral

Many centers have preprinted forms for recording both consult requests and the actual consultations. If some demographic information isn't provided initially, it can be added after the consult has been completed. Having as much data as possible beforehand increases the effectiveness of your preparation and interview. The following mnemonic summarizes the essential information to record when a consult is requested:

"I'M SURE"

Identifying factors (name, age, gender, marital status, race, religion, occupation, etc.)
Medical problem(s)
Source of referral (referring physician and service)
Urgency (routine, urgent, emergency)
Reason for referral
Expectations of the consultee

The **identifying factors** help develop a picture of the patient. Each factor has its own clinical implications and helps tailor your preparation for the consult. These factors also have the practical advantage of helping you to recognize the patient on a busy medical or surgical ward. You may well pass the person in the hallway on the way to the consult, or need to identify him or her in a room of several people.

An awareness of the patient's **medical problem** is valuable to have before the consult.

Knowing the **source** of the referral also helps with the consult. Different services and referring physicians have expectations and idiosyncrasies that, once understood, make the process easier and more effective.

It is crucial to clarify the **urgency** of the consult. Most C-L services have a time frame for inpatient and outpatient assessments (e.g. twenty-four hours, and three days respectively). It is good practice to inform the consultee approximately when to expect your visit.

The crux of the consult is of course the **reason for referral**. This becomes "the question" that has to be answered at the end of the assessment. The most common reasons for which psychiatric consults are requested are listed below:

Common Consultation Requests

Consults are usually requested for the following reasons:

Affect or Mood Changes
• Depression, anxiety, hostility, irritability, euphoria, etc.

Behavioral Problems
• Agitation or impulsivity; aggression towards self or others
• Demanding to leave the unit; refusing treatment
• Crisis intervention (non-violent); chemical or physical restraint

Capacity Determinations and Forensic Issues
• Capacity consent to treatment (**informed consent**)
• Managing finances or making a will (**testamentary capacity**)
• Involuntary hospitalization
• Ethical issues

Coping With Medical Illness
• Difficulty accepting diagnosis and/or treatment
• Psychological Factors Affecting Medical Conditions (**PFAMC**)
• Issues regarding terminal illness (e.g. pain, bereavement, etc.)
• A maladaptive reaction to illness (e.g. excessive denial, counterphobic attitude, acute stress disorder)
• Difficulty interacting with staff members

Diagnostic Evaluation
• Veracity of complaints (e.g. investigate the possibility of factitious disorder, malingering, or a somatoform disorder)
• Diagnostic evaluation of psychological complaints

Factors Related to Personal or Psychiatric History
• Sexual abuse; child abuse; elder abuse
• Personality disorders
• Substance use disorders
• Monitoring patients with pre-existing psychiatric disorders even if there are no acute issues (i.e. increasing consultees' comfort level)

Mental Status Changes
• Delirium, dementia, psychosis, etc.

Treatment
• Psychotherapy, pharmacotherapy, or other (e.g. ECT)
• Transfer of care to an inpatient unit or outpatient program (e.g. after resuscitation and detoxification from an overdose)

Preparing for the Consult

Depending on factors such as level of training, supervisor's preferences, idiosyncrasies of the referring source, nature of the consult, and knowledge of the medical problem, some preparation may be required before interviewing the patient. This process can be seen as an interaction between four entities:

Patient

C-L Service   **Consultee**

Reason for Referral

Hospitalization Particulars
• Length of hospital stay prior to the consult request?
• How did the patient come to medical attention?

Medical/Surgical History
• Type, course, and severity of the illness
• Treatments currently being given and those being planned
• Plans for future investigations and treatment

History of the Reasons for the Consultation
• Precipitating and perpetuating factors
• Exacerbations and remissions of behavioral problems
• Possible association of changes in mental status with procedures, interventions, medications, etc.
• Was anything brought in by visitors? (e.g. ethanol, pills from home)

Medication Review
• Psychiatric complications of non-psychiatric medications (e.g. steroids, antihypertensives)
• Pre-existing conditions made worse, or new medical problems caused by psychiatric medications

Laboratory Investigation Review
• Has appropriate testing been carried out, and have the results been reported?
• Have levels been drawn for applicable medications?
• Is there an association between biochemical or hematologic abnormalities and altered mental status?

Review of Information
• Check the emergency record and all multidisciplinary notes to obtain or corroborate information
• Peruse old charts for relevant history

Interviewing the Patient

Usually the most common obstacle in conducting consults is that the patient hasn't been informed of your visit. Common reasons why referring physicians don't inform patients are:
• Didn't think of it
• Too busy
• Thought the patient wouldn't understand
• Thought someone else had done it
• Feared the patient might be offended

Approaches to Initiating the Consult

It is helpful to personally contact the referring source prior to the consult for the following reasons:

• To obtain information not provided with the request
• To clarify/verify expectations
• To get a last-minute update on the patient's condition

You will be speaking to patients who, in the majority of cases, don't know about the consult. You can use the pre-consult contact (meeting or phone call) with the referring source as an opportunity to ask if notification was given, and whether the physician will introduce you to the patient. This is ideal because it introduces the patient to a team/multidisciplinary approach to treatment. The introduction can benefit, rather than harm, the relationship between the patient and the referring physician. Reluctant consultees can be told about the benefits of a personal introduction. These are that:
• It indicates a mutual awareness that there is an emotional or psychiatric problem
• It demonstrates a willingness on the physician's part to arrange for the expertise needed to help
• It relieves primary physicians of having to deal with certain aspects of patients' care, and allows them to focus on their areas of expertise by identifying someone who will deal with these issues
• The clear majority of patients are receptive to consultations

Usually a C-L psychiatrist must independently inform patients that a consult has been requested. This creates two difficulties, first introducing the idea of the consult, and second that it is to occur at that moment. Medical/surgical wards usually have rooms for one, two, or four patients. While patients generally are receptive to psychiatric consults, they are often less keen about their roommates knowing that one has been arranged. Here are some suggestions for approaching this problem.
• Have someone (usually the patient's nurse) take him or her to a private interview room
• Introduce yourself as part of the medical or surgical team and ask if the patient would be agreeable to speaking in private where you can then give a fuller explanation
• Speak in a hushed manner to preclude others from listening
• Ask the others in the room to step out for your interview (if this is reasonable and practical)
• Introduce yourself as a psychiatric consultant and offer to conduct the interview elsewhere or at another time (which at least preserves confidentiality)

Outline of the C-L Interview

The C-L interview has some unique qualities setting it apart from a general psychiatric interview. For many patients, this is their first contact with a psychiatrist, or likely, any mental health professional. They usually have not been informed of your visit, may not agree with it, or see the rationale for why it was requested. While the patient's friends and family may, in the past, have been teasing about his or her need to see a psychiatrist, finally meeting one is still another matter.

In contrast to some other types of psychiatric interviews, the C-L interview is usually quite active and engaging. An explanation detailing your position in the hospital and interest/expertise in psychiatry is frequently appropriate and helpful. A large number of people can be involved in a patient's care on medical/surgical units. A detailed introduction is welcome, as is the opportunity to help patients match up the other names and faces to whom they have been exposed.

The following points are important to include at the beginning of the interview (though you can be flexible about the order):
• Review the patient's medical problems and progress
• State the reason for the consult
• Give an approximate idea of the length of the interview and broadly what you will be asking
• You may need to obtain permission to speak with others (family members, family doctor, community psychiatrist, etc.) in order to obtain more information
• Explain that you will have to provide a report (summary of the interview) back to the referring doctor, and you can't guarantee strict confidentiality of what the patient shares with you

In most cases, patients will speak quite readily, especially if you don't ask anything too "psychiatric" at the outset. Common approaches to focusing the interview are as follows:
• Ask what the person's emotional reaction has been to the illness
• Empathize with the degree of difficulty the person has had at work and in personal relationships
• Indicate that the referring doctor was concerned, and ask in what way the person agrees with this opinion

Priorities in Conducting Consults

1. Answer the consult question.

This is essential. Keep this first and foremost in mind as you go through your preparation and interview. If the need arises, refine the request according to the situation.

2. Ask about other areas that will yield information relevant to the admission or management of the medical illness.

Common areas that need exploration regardless of the consult request are: suicidal or homicidal ideation; capacity to consent to medical treatment (and in some cases capacity to manage finances); substance abuse.

3. Determine if the patient might benefit from ongoing psychiatric treatment (e.g. psychotherapy) for a condition that is not necessarily related to the medical illness.

This can be part of a psychiatric "review of symptoms" that takes place if time permits. For example, an anxiety disorder discovered while asking a set of routine screening questions could be treated with cognitive therapy while the person is still in hospital.

Asking about the presence of other disorders can detect some of the rarer (or least reported) psychiatric conditions, such as: phobic disorders, delusional disorders, and some personality disorders, etc. However, trying to fulfill this third aspect can have potential drawbacks. Eliciting information not directly related to the consult question raises the issue of confidentiality. Should all information be put in a consult note? Should the consult note be placed on the medical chart where all disciplines have access to it? Should there be a brief note for the chart and a detailed one for the private records of the consultee? There is also the etiquette factor of not "stealing" patients. While you have a responsibility to the patient, situations that fall in this area should be cleared with, and arranged through, the referring physician.

15. Psychiatric Emergencies

Safety Concerns in Interviews

The issue of whether mentally ill patients are more likely to be violent than those in the general population has been a cause for debate in the literature.

Some research has been conducted to combat the stigma that all psychiatric patients have a high propensity for violent acts. Methodological flaws and differences in definition make a global conclusion difficult to reach (e.g. comparing violent acts on inpatient wards vs. those occurring in the community).

However, there is no debate on the fact that patients with mental illnesses can be violent, and that all clinicians need to develop a "situational awareness" about their risk of being harmed.

A growing literature reports that violence on inpatient units is increasing. Furthermore, psychiatrists are not particularly accurate in predicting violence. While some findings have been consistently reported, they are of little use in the day-to-day management of acutely ill patients. Some facts about violence are that:

• Nurses are the most frequent victims of violence
• While violence may be relatively common, serious injuries are infrequent
• Only a small percentage of patients are repeatedly violent
• There may be a seasonal variation in the level of aggressive acts

Unfortunately, prevention of violence is not widely emphasized. Many institutions have a separate room in the emergency department or outpatient clinic for interviews, but there is little adaptation for safety concerns. Some modifications that enhance safety are:

• Bolting the desk to the floor
• Putting unbreakable glass in the doors and windows
• Removing heavy objects from the room (e.g. books, ashtrays)
• Installing doors that open both ways
• Having spacious rooms
• Installing alarm systems (panic buttons) that are readily accessible

Another frequently overlooked aspect of the interview room is seating position. Make sure you are always closest to the door. Do not allow a patient to be in a position to block your exit from the room. You can show patients into the room first, and then gesture to which seat you'd like them to occupy. Of note, if a poor therapeutic alliance develops in the first interview there is a significantly higher chance of a violent act occurring.

In emergency situations, it is advisable that at least two staff members sit in on the interview. If this is not possible, inform others that you are going to conduct an interview and ask them to check in on you. Hospital security or police officers can also be present during your assessment (preferably just outside the room). You cannot conduct a good interview if you are distracted by safety concerns.

Even in cases where the sounds of an assault will be heard, other hospital staff may be reluctant to intrude or may take a few minutes to clue in to the situation. The following checklists can decrease the likelihood of an assault in an emergency setting:

A/ Prior to seeing the patient, assess the acuteness of the situation to ensure that this does not develop into an emergency for you:
• Be aware of the security arrangements that are available; attend to your safety
• Can the police or security guards be in attendance or nearby?
• Read the emergency chart
• Peruse the patient's hospital file for pertinent information
• How was the patient brought to the hospital? (e.g. police, friends, on his or her own)
• Is the patient intoxicated, restrained, or being held involuntarily?
• Has blood work been drawn? (e.g. for medication toxicity)
• Is an overdose or head trauma suspected?
• Is someone available to provide collateral history?
• Do the emergency staff have additional information?

B/ When seeing the patient, remember that the mental status of the patient is of paramount importance. Patients who have perceptual abnormalities, formal thought disorders, or delusions are the most likely to become dangerous. The following suggestions can help minimize the risk of violence:

- Sit next to the door, but don't block the exit should the patient bolt
- Give explanations for your actions and demonstrate openness
- Allow adequate, even ample, space for patients
- Don't challenge the patient's beliefs, especially at the start
- Respect the patient's autonomy
- Tell patients when you feel threatened; maintain composure
- Stress that thoughts and feelings are verbalized, not acted upon
- Be attuned to your feelings; don't react with anger or sarcasm
- Clearly document your interventions and the reasons for them

Diagnoses Most Commonly Associated With Violence
"MADS & BADS"

Mania – due to impulsivity, grandiosity, and psychotic symptoms
Alcohol – intoxication and withdrawal states
Dementia – diminished judgment and behavioral disinhibition
Schizophrenia – due to command hallucinations or delusions

Borderline personality disorder – intense anger, unstable emotions
Antisocial personality disorder – disregard for the safety of others
Delirium – hallucinations or delusions can cause violent reactions
Substance use – intoxication, particularly with hallucinogens

Assessment of Violence Risk
"ARM PAIN"

Altered state of consciousness (e.g. delirium, intoxication)
Repeated attacks – history of violence
Male gender

Paranoia (in schizophrenia, mania, or delusional disorder)
Age – more likely to be violent if younger and impulsive
Incapacity – due to brain injury, mental retardation or psychosis
Neurologic diseases – e.g. Huntington's chorea, dementia

Assessing Suicidal Risk

The following mnemonic covers the key elements in assessing suicidal risk:

"SADDLE SORE WOMAN"

Social isolation
Age
Disturbance in interpersonal relationships (**DIRs**)
Drug use/abuse
Lethality of method
Ethanol use

Sex (gender)
Occupation
Repeated attempts
Event – acute precipitant

Will – created or altered
Organic condition – chronic medical illness
Mental illness
Antidepressants, **A**kathisia
Note written

Social Isolation. Suicide rates are higher for people who live alone, which includes those who are widowed, divorced, separated, or have never been married (before listing this as a risk factor, it is important to know if it is a patient's choice to live alone). Relationships are to a large degree protective against self-harm. However, someone may be married, living with a partner, or involved in a relationship and still feel isolated.

Age is a factor because certain age groups are statistically correlated with a higher risk of completed suicides. As a general rule, the prevalence of suicide increases with age. This trend clearly develops in men starting at about age 45, and climbs continually, with a peak at age 75. Women have a later onset, starting around age 55 but exhibit a less dramatic rise with age. The elderly have a suicide rate triple that of younger people, and commit one-quarter of all suicides (yet encompass only one-tenth of the population). There is an important exception to this trend. The suicide rate among males aged 15-24 is disproportionately high (especially among whites). In this age group, suicide is consistently reported to be either the second or third most common cause of death (with accidents and homicide being the other causes).

Disturbed Interpersonal Relationships (DIRs) Disruptions in meaningful relationships provide perhaps the best answer as to *why* people take their lives. **DIRs** are one of the most common, if not the major cause of visits to emergency rooms for crisis situations. DIRs in particular refer to:
• The threat of rejection or abandonment
• Loss of approval, acceptance, affection, or attachment

Drug use/abuse is highly correlated with the likelihood of acts of self-harm. It has been estimated that the presence of chemical dependence increases the risk of completed suicide by five times that of someone who is not using drugs. The lethality of the drugs used (or available) needs to be taken into consideration. Those with the greatest potential to cause death are:
• Amphetamines
• Barbiturates
• Cocaine
• Opioids

Lethality of the method is another factor that bears on the risk of suicide. In general, the more lethal the means, the more likely it will be carried out. Males tend to use violent methods, such as weapons, jumping, and hanging. Females are more likely to take overdoses, drown, or asphyxiate themselves. The availability of firearms has been shown to have an impact on the suicide rate.

Ethanol use can lead to problems during intoxication or withdrawal states. This can be considered as part of drug use/abuse (but a vowel was needed for the mnemonic). Alcohol deserves special mention because it is the substance most often associated with acts of violence. Ethanol causes disinhibition and removes the self-restraint that would otherwise be present. The combination of impaired judgment and a greater propensity to take action has dire consequences. It is common in emergency rooms to have intoxicated patients who are combative or self-destructive, yet become entirely different when sober.

Sex (gender) is unevenly distributed for attempts and completed suicides. In all age ranges, males commit suicide more frequently than females. The ratio varies from a factor of 2:1 to almost 10:1 depending on the age group and race. Two factors help explain the gender discrepancy. As outlined in the 'L' (lethality) section, males use more lethal methods. The time course of an overdose, asphyxiation, or drowning allows an intervention to be made. Secondly, males have a higher prevalence of chemical dependency. In North America, the ratio of males to females with alcohol problems is at least 4:1. In other areas of the world it is considerably higher.

Occupation in general is a protective factor. Higher socio-economic status is associated with higher risk (though a recent change in status is also a risk factor). A possible explanation is that a higher level of occupation generally requires increased responsibility. If things go awry, affected individuals may face consequences from many avenues (e.g. marital, legal, financial, etc.)

Repeated attempts at self-harm increase the risk of a completed suicide. A distinction needs to be made between past serious, unsuccessful attempts and chronic thoughts of suicide or gestures of self-harm. The latter occurrence is called **parasuicide** and refers to chronic self-mutilation, persistent thoughts or threats of suicide, or non-lethal attempts.

Events of an acute nature increase the risk of suicide. The presence of *loss* is central to precipitants that lead to suicidal behavior. This can be a perceived or actual loss of love, esteem, wealth, health, fame, etc. The most common event leading to the wish to die is a disturbance in an interpersonal relationship (**DIR**). In situations where a precipitant is not obvious, consideration of three other factors may help shed some light:

1. In some cases, people react to a symbolic loss rather than an actual one. Exploring the meaning of apparently minor events can help identify the precipitant.

2. People may not be consciously aware of what influences them. For example, watching a movie or hearing a song can bring about associations that evoke painful memories.

3. **Anniversary reactions** occur on the dates of major losses. Some patients may be completely unaware of why they are suicidal at a certain point in time. An exploration of dates significant to that person may reveal this as the cause.

Wills and **Notes** indicate that planning was involved in the attempt, which is correlated with an increased risk of completion. Patients who wish to "tidy up their affairs" may have Wills created or altered. While the contents of a Will are confidential, many patients make reference to it prior to a suicide attempt. Generally, notes either act as a way of telling others what the person thought of them, or as a plea to those left behind to understand why the suicide occurred.

Organic conditions (general medical conditions) can be risk factors due to their seriousness or chronicity. This is also one of the reasons why suicide is more prevalent among the elderly.

Mental Illness is the strongest risk factor associated with suicide. Over 90% of those who take their own lives have a diagnosable mental condition at the time of death. The presence of a mental illness is estimated to increase the risk of committing suicide tenfold. The majority of patients who commit suicide have seen a physician within six months of dying, and frequently within one month. Other studies have found that a high percentage of patients who took their lives had been given a prescription for a psychotropic medication. Among psychiatric disorders, mood disorders and alcohol abuse (respectively) are the conditions that have the highest association with suicide.

Antidepressants. Recovery from depression tends to follow a pattern of vegetative symptoms first, then cognitive functions, and lastly, mood symptoms and suicidal thoughts. This can place patients in the situation where they have a return of energy but still have thoughts of self-harm. **Akathisia** is a restlessness or "squirreliness" (usually due to antipsychotic use) that causes patients to feel they must keep moving. Akathisia can be very distressing, and some patients have taken their lives rather than endure this unpleasant feeling.

16. The Mini-Mental State Exam (MMSE)

The Folstein Mini-Mental State Exam

Orientation
Score
• What is the – (day) (date) (month) (season) (year)? / 5
• Where are you now?   (building) (floor) (town)
(state) (country) / 5

Registration
• List 3 objects at one-second intervals, then ask
the patient to repeat all 3; give one point for each
correct answer given on the first trial; repeat this
until the patient can recite all 3 items / 3

Attention/Concentration
• Serial 7's Test up to 5 subtractions (starting with
100 – 7); alternatively ask the patient to spell
"WORLD" backwards (D - L - R - O - W) / 5

Recall
• Ask the patient to recite the above 3 items / 3

Language
• Show the patient a watch and a pen and ask the
patient to name these items / 2

• Ask the patient to repeat the following statement:
"No ifs, ands, or buts." / 1

• Ask the patient to follow these commands:
"Take a piece of paper in your right hand." (1 pt.)
"Fold it in half." (1 pt.)
"Place it on the floor." (1 pt.) / 3

• Read and follow this command:
"Close your eyes." / 1

Score

• Write a sentence:

_____

_____

_____

_____

/ 1

• Copy the following diagram:

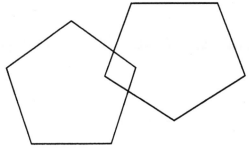

/ 1

Total Score

/ 30

What is the Mini-Mental State Exam?

The **Mini-Mental State Exam (MMSE)** is a structured clinical assessment of cognitive functioning. It was published by Dr. M. Folstein et al* in 1975 and has been referred to as "The Folstein Test" or the "Folstein MMSE." The MMSE provides a quantified assessment of various dimensions of cognitive functioning. The original article does not describe time limits for giving this test. The usual time required for administering this test is from three to five minutes.

The test is scored out of a maximum thirty points. An average score for patients without cognitive impairment is twenty-eight. Scores of twenty-four or less indicate than an abnormality is present, which is usually dementia or delirium. The MMSE is one of many screening tests used to detect and monitor cognitive impairment.

* M. Folstein, S. Folstein & P. McHugh
Mini-Mental State: A Practical Method for Grading the Cognitive State of Patients for the Clinician
Journal of Psychiatric Research 12: p. 189 – 198, 1975
Reprinted with permission.

Instructions for Administering the MMSE

Orientation
• Ask for the date, then ask specifically for parts omitted (e.g. season, year)
• Ask patients to tell you exactly where they are now, then ask for the parts omitted (state, country, etc.)

Registration
• Ask if you may test memory, then list 3 unrelated objects in a clear voice with about 1 second between each item. After giving the list once, ask the patient to repeat this list and score 1 point for each item on this trial. Because you will be testing recall later, continue to give patients the list of objects until they can repeat them fully. If patients are unable to repeat these items after 6 trials, they cannot be meaningfully tested.

Attention and Concentration

• Ask patients to begin with 100 and count backwards by 7. Stop after 5 subtractions (93, 86, 79, 72, 65). Score the total number of correct answers. If patients can't or won't perform this task, ask them to spell the word "world" backwards.

The score is the number of letters in correct order, e.g., dlrow = 5, dlorw = 3, dolrw = 2, dolwr = 1, world = 0

Recall

• Ask patients to recall the 3 words you previously asked them to remember. Score 0 – 3.

Language

• Naming: Show patients a wrist watch and ask them to name it. Repeat for a pen or pencil. Score 0 – 2.

• Repetition: Ask the patient to repeat the sentence after you. Allow only one trial. Score 0 or 1.

• 3-Stage command: Use blank paper and repeat the command. Score 1 point for each part correctly executed.

• Reading: On a blank piece of paper print the sentence "Close your eyes," in letters large enough for patients to see clearly. Ask them to read it and do what it says. Score 1 point only if the eyes are closed.

• Writing: Give patients a blank piece of paper and ask them to write a sentence for you. Do not dictate a sentence, it is to be written spontaneously. It must contain a subject and verb and be sensible. Correct grammar and punctuation aren't necessary.

Copying

On a clean piece of paper, draw intersecting pentagons, each side about 1 in., and ask the patient to copy it exactly as it is. All 10 angles must be present and the pentagons must intersect to score 1 point. Tremor and rotation are ignored.

Critique of the MMSE

The following scenario plays itself out again and again –

It is the first day of a rotation in psychiatry for a group of clinical clerks. One of the keener students grabs a chart to review the presenting history before seeing the patient. After having some idea what to ask about, she tries to recall the format of a psychiatric interview. "Not much different than a standard interview," she muses, "except for this weird thing called the mental status exam." Somewhere, somehow she comes across a copy of the MMSE, and her confusion disappears. She presents the case thoroughly, and when it comes time to present the mental status, she smiles and says, "On the mental status exam, the patient scored 26."

The major pitfall of the MMSE is that it is NOT the same as a complete mental status exam. The similarity in names is certainly part of the confusion. The MMSE was designed to be a rapid screening instrument for cognitive impairment, and has three main clinical applications:

• It tests features that are often omitted in traditional mental status exams, such as reading, writing, copying, repetition, following commands, and detailed questions about orientation

• On the basis of the score from the initial test, it is useful for screening for dementia and delirium (e.g. a score less than 24 indicates impairment)

• It provides a quantifiable score to follow the day-to-day progress of a patient in hospital

The MMSE does not include many of the features assessed by a thorough MSE. It can certainly be a useful addition, but it is by no means a replacement. The MMSE is the most popular psychiatric screening assessment and has a large body of literature supporting its use. The validity of MMSE scores have been demonstrated through positive correlations with performance on intelligence tests and deficits found on brain imaging.

The MMSE is more specific that it is sensitive. An abnormal score is highly suggestive of cognitive impairment, though patients with mild dementia or delirium often score higher than twenty-five on the test. Patients with little formal education may have spuriously low scores. Another pitfall involves patients who develop dementia but who had a superior level of intelligence. Such patients continue to have normal scores on the MMSE despite their progressive deficits.

Studies have shown the MMSE to have a high reliability both between interviewers, and on successive days with the same interviewer.

17. Medicolegal Principles*

* Much of the material in this chapter is condensed from:

Medicolegal Issues in Clinical Practice:
A Primer for the Legally Challenged
by Deborah J. Wear-Finkle MD, MPA
ISBN 1-894328-08-6
Published by Rapid Psychler Press

Ethics & Law

Ethics
• principles of proper or morally correct behavior within a society

 If enough people in a society support an ethical principle, it can become a law.

Law
• the rules of conduct as established by a society

Ethical principles are enforced by regulatory bodies (i.e. State medical boards). These boards can revoke a physician's license even if a law hasn't been broken. Legal principles are enforced by the courts.

Medical Ethics

The two primary principles of medical ethics are:

Autonomy – the right of every competent person to be able to decide what treatment he or she will accept

Beneficence – known simply as "do good for the patient" (also known as **nonmalfeasance** – *Do No Harm*)

The preamble from the **1999 AMA Code of Medical Ethics** states that: *"The medical profession has long subscribed to a body of ethical statements developed primarily for the benefit of the patient. As a member of this profession, a physician must recognize responsibility not only to patients, but also to society, to other health professionals, and to self."* The following seven principles adopted by the AMA are not laws, but standards of conduct which define honorable behavior for physicians.

1. A physician shall be dedicated to providing competent medical service with compassion and respect for human dignity.

2. A physician shall deal honestly with patients and colleagues, and strive to expose those physicians deficient in character or competence, or who engage in fraud or deception.

3. A physician shall respect the law, and also recognize a responsibility to seek changes in those requirements which are contrary to the best interests of the patient.

4. A physician shall respect the rights of patients, of colleagues, and of other health professionals, and shall safeguard patient confidences within the constraints of the law.

5. A physician shall continue to study, apply, and advance scientific knowledge, make relevant information available to patients, colleagues, and the public, obtain consultation, and use the talents of other health professionals when indicated.

6. A physician shall, in the provision of appropriate patient care, except in emergencies, be free to choose whom to serve, with whom to associate, and the environment in which to provide medical services.

7. A physician shall recognize a responsibility to participate in activities contributing to an improved community.

Types of Law

There are two basic types of law in Canada and the U.S. – criminal and civil. The goal of **criminal law** is to effect justice and to dispense punishment for crimes committed. The aim of **civil law** is to make restitution to the wronged party, or "to make whole again," which usually involves a financial penalty.

A **tort** is any civil wrong against another person. Tort law covers civil actions between two parties, which are defined as either *intentional* or *unintentional torts*. **Intentional torts** are deliberate actions which may cause damage. They are not usually covered by malpractice insurance. Examples include: assault and battery, sexual relationships with patients, and false imprisonment. **Unintentional torts** are actions that possess an unreasonable risk of causing harm. Medical malpractice falls under this broader area of negligence law.

Medical Negligence

The 4 D'S

There are four components required for a negligence action to be considered valid. The four D's that a plaintiff must establish for a successful negligence suit are:

• **Duty** (of a doctor to a patient)
• **Dereliction** of duty, or a deviation from the standard of care
• **Direct Causation** of the problem
• **Damage** (an injury was caused)

For a negligence suit to be considered, some form of injury (physical or emotional) must be present. If not, a lawsuit cannot be launched, even if a physician has blatantly violated accepted standards of care. On the other hand, an unfavorable outcome for one of your patients does not mean you will automatically be sued. Depending on your specialty and the acuity level of your patients, there is the ever-present risk of unfavorable outcomes. When they occur, it does not reflect on you as a physician – uncertainty is an integral part of medical practice.

First, a duty must be established. A **duty** to a patient begins any time there is a **doctor-patient relationship (DPR)**. When a DPR is established, the doctor has a duty to provide a certain **standard of care (SOC)** for that patient. If there is evidence that the SOC is breached, a dereliction of the duty is considered to have occurred, which is the next link necessary in a successful malpractice action. The final step involves demonstrating that the deviation from the SOC was the direct causation of the patient's injury.

Standard of Proof

Each of the four elements in alleged negligence cases must be proven to a specific legal standard. The legal standard of proof required in negligence cases in almost all jurisdictions is called a **preponderance of evidence**. This is considered to be "more likely than not" or, for those who think numerically, this is a 51% degree of certainty. With very few exceptions, the plaintiff in a malpractice claim must show, with a *preponderance of evidence*, that the alleged negligence was the defendant's responsibility. The majority of civil cases use preponderance of evidence as the legal standard.

Other legal standards exist. The next highest standard of proof is called that of **clear and convincing evidence**. This is used in civil cases where there is a more substantial right at risk (rather than mere monetary remuneration), such as someone's liberty (as in a civil commitment), or the right of a hospitalized psychiatric patient to refuse medication. The clear and convincing standard is considered to be somewhere in the vicinity of 75 – 85% certainty.

The highest standard of proof is called **beyond a reasonable doubt**, and is considered to be level of certainty of about 95%. This standard is applied in criminal cases and in some jurisdictions for specific civil actions. To believe something beyond a reasonable doubt means "you better be darn sure!"

Duty
Duty to a patient is established by formally providing medical services (such as assignment to your primary care panel or in a consultation). It can also be implied, as in working in an emergency room (ER) and treating patients seeking care there.

Situations that are less clear might involve a neighbor requesting your medical advice. The law presumes that when a physician provides some form of evaluation/treatment, even informally, a duty to that person has been established. You may want to rethink the "cocktail party consult" the next time you are asked for your advice – or at least be very circumspect in your comments. It is safe to say something like "That's a good question – I think you should contact your doctor about this matter as it is not really appropriate for me to give you advice."

Once a DPR has been is established, the physician has the duty to provide the SOC for that patient.

Direct Causation
Determining cause in malpractice cases generally involves two factors:
• **Cause-in-fact**, which refers to whether "but for" the alleged act, the injury would not have occurred

• **Proximate cause**, which is a substantial factor in the resultant injury; this also is related to the term of *foreseeability*

Damage

Any successful medical malpractice lawsuit must show that some type of injury was sustained. Such "damage" is usually a compensable injury or a death that occurs because of a specific act or omission. The most common types of acts or omissions include:
• Incorrect diagnosis
• Delays in making a diagnosis or instituting treatment
• Providing inappropriate treatment
• Medication side-effects or errors
• Procedural errors

Standard of Care

The **standard of care (SOC)** is defined as *practicing with the same reasonable level of skill that a prudent physician with similar training and experience would recognize as adequate and acceptable in similar circumstances*. Readers are encouraged to check with local medical practice statutes for exact definitions. With few exceptions, the SOC is based on national standards, not local ones. The definition of SOC does not necessarily specify the best, most expensive, or technologically advanced care that can be provided. Rather, it refers to care that is considered "acceptable" and "adequate" to similarly trained practitioners working under similar circumstances.

When using medications, be careful if you are prescribing something for a non-approved use. Always state your rationale, which should be supportable by peer review references. In the U.S. the **Physicians Desk Reference (PDR)**, and in Canada the **Compendium of Pharmaceutical Specialties (CPS)** has been used as the SOC in several cases when a drug was used in a dosage outside the recommended range, or for a different duration of treatment. You can use a drug in ways that you believe are appropriate as long as you document your reasons.

Alternative Treatments

There are many alternative treatments available (i.e. herbal medicines, acupuncture, etc.). Rather than discuss the various merits of these approaches, a caution will be given:
If there is evidence that you prescribed an alternative treatment that allegedly led to an injury, you will not be seen as having met the SOC if other prudent, similarly trained and experienced physicians, would not also consider this treatment in a similar situation.

Informed Consent

Probably the most important communication issue that occurs between physicians and patients involves **informed consent (IC)**. While IC is well established as both an ethical and legal right of patients, its importance to successful DPRs cannot be overemphasized. Autonomy and the right of self-determination of each person are the fundamental ethical principles that apply to medical practice. These principles are at the very heart of medical ethics, and can assist decision-making in difficult areas of practice.

The practice of sharing uncertainty with patients is crucial in medical decision-making. IC means a two-way communication, and is never merely a signature on a piece of paper. Clinicians who are comfortable with the IC process respect the autonomy of their patients. Respecting autonomy means that practitioners must *know and understand* what their patients want, not *assume* to know what they would want in any particular situation.

IC is a legal and ethical doctrine that requires healthcare professionals to inform patients about their diagnoses, and the risks and benefits of various treatment options. Once it is clear that patients understand these aspects, they are allowed to make their choices, and clinicians must respect these decisions.

The Process of Obtaining IC

1. The patient is deemed to be capable of making medical decisions for himself (unless determined to be otherwise)

2. The patient is free of overt and covert coercion

3. The patient is fully informed about the following areas:
• The diagnosis and its implications
• The risks and benefits of the course of treatment being recommended
• The risks and benefits of alternative treatments
• The risks and benefits of receiving no treatment

The principle of **shared uncertainty** cannot be overemphasized. Almost everything that happens in medicine involves at least some degree of uncertainty. If patients understand the relative degree of uncertainty they face, they are much more likely to also accept the setbacks that may occur. Sharing uncertainty also distributes the responsibility between the patient and the physician on a more equal basis. Readers are reminded to check their local laws regarding their exact requirements for obtaining IC. When addressing IC issues with patients, a guiding principle is to consider what you would want the doctor to tell you, your spouse, parent, sibling, etc. about any particular diagnosis or choice of treatment. Note that the responsibility for obtaining IC from the patient cannot be delegated (even to another physician).

Documenting Informed Consent
• Good notes do help the patient
• If you didn't document it – "it" never happened
• Write smarter, not more
• If it can't be read, it won't help you or anyone else

Capacity Assessments

For IC to be considered valid, the person giving it must be competent to do so. All adults are presumed to be competent unless there is a legitimate reason to think otherwise. The underlying assumption is that the person considering treatment is able to do so under the umbrella of protection provided by the ethical and legal doctrine of **self-determination**. Because of this, many physicians don't mention that the patient was deemed competent when IC was obtained. Making a notation in the medical record that a patient was deemed capable of providing IC can be very beneficial.

Competence refers to having the capacity to understand and act reasonably. Competence is a legal term, and the decision about someone's competence is made by a judge.

Capacity is having the mental ability to make a rational decision (based on understanding and appreciating all relevant information). Capacity is determined by a clinician.

There are many different types of capacity assessments (over 30) that can be adjudged. In general, when there is more at stake for an individual (e.g. loss of life or liberty, finances, etc.), a higher level of evidence indicating competence is required.

Areas of Competence/Capacity

This list is compiled in approximate decreasing order of stringency:
• Execution

• Stand Trial – the accused must understand what he is being charged with, the role of the major figures in the courtroom (i.e. what the jury does, etc.), and be able to participate in his or her own defense

• Be Sentenced

• Manage Financial Affairs – a person must know the basics of what something costs, how items are paid for, the general nature of their assets, etc., although it is not required that the person makes sound financial decisions

• Live Independently – the person must be able to list the important aspects of how to live safely on his or her own (i.e. how to find a place to stay, how to find food, remember to turn off the stove, etc.)

• Make Medical Decisions

• Enter Into a Contract – this requires an understanding of what a contract involves, and what is at risk

• Be A Witness (**Testimonial Capacity**) – this often becomes an issue when a child is required to give testimony

• Get Married – this requires an understanding of what marriage means, and the general responsibilities required of a spouse

• Vote – political commentary aside. . . albeit tempting

• Make A Will (**Testamentary Capacity**) – this involves one of the lowest standards of evidence. In general, a person's wishes are carried out as long as there was no coercion or undue influence at the time the will was written. Testamentary capacity requires: that the person knows a will is being made; an approximate understanding of net worth; identity of the natural heirs; and in some jurisdictions, an understanding of the potential impact that financial decisions would have on the "usual" heirs.

Each of these "competencies" are assessed by balancing an individual's rights against local laws and the interests of society.

In most jurisdictions, attending physicians are legally able to be the "capacity assessors" for their patients. However, the majority of physicians, unless trained in the assessment process, do not understand how to proceed, and are wise to request assistance. When a consultant (usually a psychiatrist or psychologist) is asked to "do a capacity assessment," it is important to clarify which type of capacity needs to be assessed, and for what specific reason. These are crucial elements, because "capacity" is specific to a person's decision-making ability for a *specific task* at a *specific time*. (e.g. to assess Mr. Langerhan's capacity to consent to an ERCP scheduled for tomorrow). There are mental health professionals who do not know how to conduct capacity assessments. For this reason, it is prudent to ensure that your consult request is directed to someone who has the proper training and experience.

An error frequently made by clinicians is to equate a patient's decision-making capacity with her performance on the **MMSE**. While most researchers agree that scores of less than 20 (out of 30) on the MMSE provide a fairly good correlation with a lack of decision-making capacity, this alone is not sufficient evidence. Also, up to one-third of patients with impairments in their decision-making ability (overlooked by physicians) will score between 20 – 30 on the MMSE.

The capacity to make medical decisions balances the competing interests of doing no harm to the patient against preserving the right to self-determination. The principle underlying the concept of IC is that each person, while deemed competent, has the right to make decisions regarding his or her medical care, even if others consider these decisions to be unwise. This principle is at times difficult for physicians to accept. Many authors who write in the area of medical decision-making capacity believe in the usefulness of a "sliding scale," where different types of capacity require varying levels of decision-making ability. In other words, the more there is at risk for the patient, the more physicians will want to be certain that the patient has intact decision-making capacity. While a sliding scale is not an officially recognized legal consideration, it does have widespread acceptance.

A Method for Assessing the Capacity for Consent to Treatment

Suggested Procedure for Determining Capacity
• Inform the patient of the reason for your visit/assessment
• Inform the patient of his or her diagnosis
• Outline the risks and benefits of your proposed treatment
• Outline the risks and benefits of alternate treatments
• Explain the risks and likely consequences of receiving no treatment
• Use plain English!
• Ask the patient to repeat what his or her understanding is of the situation, and what he or she heard you say
• Perform a mental status exam (it is especially important to test orientation, thought content & process, perception and cognition)
• Document the patient's responses

Assess the Following to Determine Capacity
• What is the patient's choice?
• What is the patient's rationale for making that choice?
• What are the likely consequences of exercising the choice?
• Can the patient weigh the pros and cons of various alternatives?
• What is the patient's understanding of the medical problem?
• What is the patient's understanding of your recommendations and rationale?
• What consequences does the patient foresee from the treatment you have proposed?
• What consequences does the patient foresee from NOT receiving treatment?
• Can the patient make a commitment to a choice?

If You Deem the Patient Incapable
• Document your interaction with the patient completely
• Inform the patient (verbally and in writing)
• Ask for a second opinion (colleague, psychiatrist)
• Ask for legal advice (lawyer, rights advisor)
• Involve the family as soon and as completely as possible
• Obtain substitute consent before proceeding

A Method for Assessing Financial Capacity

Preparing for the Interview

• Establish a diagnosis, differential diagnosis, treatment plan, and prognosis for the patient.
• Obtain as much information about the patient's financial matters as possible.
• Are there any documented problems with estate management?
• What is the patient's usual style of money management?
• Has power of attorney been assigned or a substitute decision maker designated?
• Obtain or make arrangements for collateral information from family members, relevant professionals, and business associates.

Conducting the Interview

• Inform the patient of the reason for the assessment.
• Inform the patient of his or her diagnosis and prognosis.
• Ask the patient for his or her understanding of the above factors and document these responses.

General Inquiries

• What is the patient's appreciation of the consequences of being financially incompetent?
• What is the patient's understanding of power of attorney, substitute decision maker, and the function of a Guardian?
• Can the patient accurately give the costs of common items and expenses?
• Can the patient describe common banking procedures?

Specific Inquiries

• What consequences does the patient foresee in terms of how financial mismanagement would affect himself or herself, family members, creditors, etc.? Who else would be affected by poor financial judgment, and to what extent? Is the patient's occupation one that involves dealing with other people's finances? Is this seen as a potential source of difficulty, and to what extent?
• What is the patient's knowledge of sources of income, assets, property, investments, etc?

• What is the patient's awareness of debts and ongoing expenses?
• Ask for specific figures to corroborate collateral information.
• What are the immediate plans for financial expenditures? Can the patient commit to a definite plan?
• How would the patient go about implementing the above plan?
• Are there other options that the patient is able to consider? What are the foreseeable consequences of these options?
• What is the rationale for the chosen course of action?
• What are the patient's wishes regarding estate management?
• How well does the patient cope with daily financial tasks?
• Is the patient aware of having any difficulties with management of his or her finances?
• Has the assistance of the family or community supports been required in the past? What support is available on an ongoing basis? What is the patient's attitude towards using resources to help with financial matters?
• Who does the patient consider to be a trustworthy source of assistance for financial matters?

Interventions Following from Interview Findings
• Clearly document the findings from your interview, the results of cognitive testing and the details from other sources of information used in making your decision about capacity.
• Inform the patient of the results of your determination. Some jurisdictions require particular forms be given to patients as official notification of financial incapacity.
• In accordance with local laws, inform the necessary parties of the finding of incapacity and implement the least restrictive process that protects the patient's estate.

Ten Commandments for Legally Aware Physicians*

I.   Thou shalt practice within thy scope of training, experience, and privileging.

II.   Thou shalt never place thy needs above thine patient's, and avoideth all personal relationships with those whom you treat.

III. Thou shalt never promiseth a result.

IV.   Thou shalt document what thou hast done (concisely, precisely, and legibly).

V.   Thou shalt ensureth proper informed consent, and discloseth all treatment options.

VI.   Thou shalt maketh every attempt to listen to thine patients and attempt to empathize, even with the unlikable.

VII. Thou shalt ensureth proper professional liability insurance coverage (which includeth administrative actions).

VIII. Thou shalt consult with legal counsel at all times when it is appropriate to do so.

IX.   Thou shalt demonstrate humility.

X.   Thou shalt knoweth thine state laws and local policies.

This page may be copied and freely circulated.

* From the book:

Medicolegal Issues in Clinical Practice:
A Primer for the Legally Challenged
by Deborah J. Wear-Finkle MD, MPA
ISBN 1-894328-08-6
Published by Rapid Psychler Press

18. A Case Presentation

Author's Note

In order to provide a useful case summary that has wide applicability as a teaching tool, I have chosen to base it on a movie. This has several advantages:
• Videos are an excellent instructional medium and provide more information than a written case summary
• The subject of the film has chosen to share his experiences with the world, thereby removing concerns about confidentiality
• Readers get access to all the information, and can watch the movie at their leisure

From the many superb films with psychiatric content, I have chosen to discuss the movie *Shine*, which was released in 1996 and is widely available on videotape and DVD. However, prior to presenting this material, I would like to make the following disclaimers about the presentation that follows.

Disclaimer #1

I am offering an opinion on how the main character's role reflects signs and symptoms of psychiatric illness. I am clearly NOT offering an opinion on the real person's condition. I have done no supplemental reading, read no case reports, and have interviewed none of the people whose lives are portrayed in the movie. I ask you to please keep in mind that because of the artistic license taken by filmmakers, the main character may be affected by quite a different illness than what is shown in the film, and indeed, may suffer from no illness at all. In this particular film, many people (including the main character's sister, Margaret Helfgott) have taken issue with the portrayal of David and his father, Peter). For this reason, I am discussing this movie as a fictionalized version of actual events.

Disclaimer #2

For ease of identification, I have used the name of the actors as well as the name of the character being portrayed. Again, I am offering an opinion on how close the portrayal is to a "real" patient. I am not giving an opinion on the quality of the performance. I am also most certainly not making comments on the actors' personal lives.

Disclaimer #3

Mental health professionals spend years in training to be able to distinguish the signs and symptoms of psychiatric illnesses, and to be able to coalesce these findings into an accurate diagnosis. There is no shortcut to this process. Anyone professing any expertise solely from the material in this book is doing themselves a disservice as well as the person being offered the opinion. I consider such a short-cut akin to reading a book about swimming and then trying to cross a lake (and drowning).

Disclaimer #4

I am not a world-renowned diagnostician. A fertile discussion could ensue from the material presented here, no doubt generating a lengthy list of possible diagnoses. For the purposes of clarity and brevity, I have chosen to focus on what appears to me to be the principal diagnosis, and then note features that are less common or inconsistent.

'Shine'

Country of Origin: Australia   **Release Date:** 1996
Rated: PG-13
U.S. Distributor: FineLine Features/New Line Cinema
Cast: Geoffrey Rush (adult David Helfgott)
Noah Taylor (adolescent David Helfgott)
Alex Rafalowicz (child David Helfgott)
Armin Mueller-Stahl (Elias Peter Helfgott, David's father)
Director: Scott Hicks   **Screenplay:** Scott Hicks, Jan Sardi
Awards: Scores of nominations and many awards, including 6 Oscar nominations, and Best Actor Award for Geoffrey Rush

Books:
Love You to Bits and Pieces: Life With David Helfgott
by Gillian Helfgott with Alissa Tanskaya
ISBN 0140266445
Published by Penguin, 1997

Out of Tune: David Helfgott and the Myth of Shine
by Margaret Helfgott with Tom Gross
ISBN 0446523836
Published by Warner Books, 1998

Introduction to 'Shine'

Shine follows the life of child piano prodigy David Helfgott. The movie takes place in Australia and England. In the opening scene, we see a man stumbling around in a heavy rain. He happens upon a wine bar called Moby's and, seeing a piano, bangs on the locked door until a sympathetic staff member lets him in. The man is able to say that his name is David, but otherwise has a style of speaking that is very difficult to follow. His unusual speech pattern at times lacks clear connections between ideas, and on other occasions contains puns and references which are off topic (but can be understood as being related to some central theme). David demonstrates a persistently jovial mood, and bobs around the bar seeking hugs.

The movie then flashes back to David's childhood. He is at a music recital and has already earned some acclaim (judging by the enthusiasm of the attendees as he approaches the stage). One of the judges (one of David's future teachers) notices his talent. Shortly afterwards, we discover that he lost the competition (because the piano was rolling across the stage). David's father, Peter, is a powerful figure – at times teeming with affection and at other times unable to control his rage. As a boy, Peter cherished a violin that his father smashed. Perhaps as an act of defiance, Peter trained his children to play the piano. Peter lost his family in a Polish concentration camp and is determined to keep his family together at any cost. The viewer is thus introduced to the principal conflict in David's life – nurture his prodigious talent, or acquiese to his father's demands that he not leave the family. Peter almost fanatically drives David to win competitions, but impedes his progress by rebuffing teachers and burning scholarship offers.

Ultimately, David must leave Australia for England to perfect his craft. We see him at the Royal College of Music under the tutelage of a talented and sympathetic professor (played by John Gielgud). Just as David finishes performing a monstrously difficult piece (Rachmaninoff's Piano Concerto No. 3) he collapses, and spends the next decade in hospitals and hostels. We first see him as an adult in the scene described at the top of this page. The presentation begins as if the staff from the wine bar took him to hospital instead of returning him to his residence. For the sake of completeness, some historical details were inserted by the author.

Case Presentation

Identification
David is a Jewish male in his forties. He is divorced and has no children. He is unemployed and supported on social assistance.

Reason for Referral
David was brought to hospital by three employees of a wine bar. They let him in from the rain and were concerned that he had become lost. Due to David's degree of disorganization, largely incoherent speech, and lack of identification, they thought medical assistance should be sought.

History of Present Illness
Collateral history was obtained from David's landlord. For most of the day, David spends time in his room sleeping and reading sheet music. He has a piano in his room that he will practice for hours. His playing needs to be limited by the landlord (by locking the keyboard) so that the other members of the house are not disturbed. David's room is a mess, with old letters, music, and photographs strewn about. He is unable to manage his finances and signs over his check to his landlord. David sleeps on the floor. His meals are brought to him as he cannot cook for himself and often ventures out, forgetting to eat, and getting lost in the process.

David's mood is expansive. He is gregarious and seeks hugs and kisses from everyone in the room. He has a charm and energy about him, keeping a running dialogue with 'stream of consciousness' verbalizations. His rapid speech is an unusual blend of puns, metaphors, clang associations, and bits of wisdom. He offers little information spontaneously, but anything said in his presence becomes altered and reflected back. Left to his own, he appears to be focused on an inner, autistic world.

He appears to need to keep moving. David examines items around him in a clumsy manner and loses interest quickly, preferring to engage others in dialogue. He denies feeling depressed. He says his appetite, energy level, ability to concentrate, self-esteem, and libido are all OK. He denies current suicidal ideation or any past attempts; similarly he has no thoughts of wanting to hurt others.

Psychiatric History

David collapsed after performing at a music competition in England. He was given a course of ECT (6 treatments) shortly afterwards which helped him, but caused some memory problems which prevent David from giving more information about this period of time. Prior to his collapse, he was unduly focused on his playing. He became unkempt and cared little for his grooming. On one occasion he forgot to wear his pants. As a child, David had episodes of encopresis and enuresis. On one occasion he was beaten by his father for defecating in the bathtub. David is taking haloperidol 5 mg per day and oxazepam 60 mg at bedtime to help him sleep.

Medical History

David has no significant past or current medical problems.

Substance Use History

David began smoking cigarettes as a teenager and smokes continuously now (estimated at 40 per day). He drinks on a social basis and has had no addiction problems other than nicotine.

Family History

David is one of four children – he has three sisters: Suzie, Louise, and Margaret. David's father, Peter, and mother, Rachel, are still alive, though his father is ailing.

David's parents are Polish Jews who emigrated prior to World War II. He his lost paternal grandparents and maternal aunts in Nazi concentration camps. David is in touch with his sisters but has been estranged from his parents since his teens (when he left for England). Peter refused to respond to David's letters, but apparently listened to his performance on the radio and taped it as well. Peter was described as a meticulous man who was passionate about his ideas. He was guarded about his family and had few friends. Rachel was a good mother who spent her time caring for the children and preparing meals. In all but a few cases, Peter made the decisions for the household and expected everyone to abide by them.

David is uncertain about psychiatric illness in his family, but believes one of his father's siblings may have been affected.

Personal History

David was born in Melbourne, Australia on May 10, 1947. He was a term birth and weighed 7 pounds, 7 ounces. There were no complications with his delivery. He met his developmental milestones appropriately. He started school at the usual age and did very well, being a studious boy who wanted to please his father. David socialized minimally with his peers, and in particular avoided team sports.

David's father, a self-taught musician, gave him lessons on the piano starting at age three. It was clear that David had an incredible gift and rapidly developed as a player, surpassing his father's skills easily. David was able to play complex musical passages after hearing them only one or two times.

He had an endearing, innocent quality. He was very sensitive and spent most of his time indoors with his sisters. His main interests were intellectual – chess, mathematics, and philosophy. When allowed by his father, David was able to socialize with others and form some friendships, though few were very close. His most significant attachments outside his family were to his music teacher (Ben Rosen) and an older female patron (Katharine Susannah Prichard).

David was driven not only to excel at the piano, but to win competitions. When he was the runner-up in a national competition, he seemed withdrawn and flat, but was more concerned about disappointing his father than losing the competition.

David was offered a scholarship in the U.S., but his father refused to allow him to go. David was able to recall some of the things his father told him about life:
• "In this world only the strong survive. The weak get crushed like insects."
• "It is a terrible thing to hate your father. Music will always be your friend. Everything else will let you down. Life is cruel, you have to survive."
• "There is no one who will love you like me. You can't trust anyone, but I will always be there. I will be with you, for ever and ever."

When David informed his father of his scholarship to England, this was his response –
"You think you can just do as you please?" (David was then beaten)

"If you go, you will never come back into this house again. You will never be anybody's son. The girls will lose a brother. Is that what you want? You want to destroy your family? If you love me, you will stop this nonsense, you will not step out that door. If you go, you will be punished for the rest of your life. My David, don't go."

As David left the house, his father shouts after him, "Don't make me do it!" Shortly afterward, Peter burned the scrapbook he kept of David's accomplishments.

After returning from England, David called his father, but Peter hung up on him. David then spent years in boarding homes and hospitals. He gave up playing the piano, thinking that it was somehow connected with his fate. Finally, he saw a piano being played during a recreation group, and befriended Beryl, the woman playing it. Beryl was instrumental in getting David out of institutions. She was unable to tolerate his inattentiveness (leaving the television on, water running out of the bathroom, etc.). Beryl arranged for David to find his current lodgings in a boarding home with a sympathetic landlord.

Review of Symptoms
Based on the above history, symptoms were asked about the following conditions:
- Schizophrenia
- Mania
- Depression
- Early onset dementia
- Schizoid and schizotypal personality disorder

Mental Status Exam
Appearance: David is a white male who appears to be in his early forties. He is thin but not emaciated, and has tobacco stains on his right hand. He is wearing a raincoat with a shirt and trousers – all of which are soaked because he was out in the rain for hours, giving him an overall disheveled appearance.

Behavior: David paces around the interview room looking at items and commenting on them. He is the center of attention – engaging everyone around him in conversation while hugging and trying to kiss anyone he can. He gesticulates widely with his hands when speaking. He often speaks with his eyes closed. David gives the impression of someone who is curious about the people and objects around him, but is easily distracted by a short attention span.

Cooperation & Reliability: David was cooperative, but so distractible that this interfered with the interview. He seems to mean well when answering questions. Because of his memory difficulties and thought process abnormalities, the information provided from David directly was deemed to be of only moderate reliability.

Speech: David's speech was spontaneous and fluent. He speaks rapidly with an Australian accent. He doesn't articulate all of his words carefully and at times is incoherent because of his pressure of speech.

Thought Form/Process: This is David's most striking mental status finding. He has a rambling speech pattern that at times can be understood to be around a central theme (flight of ideas), and at other times the connection between ideas is lost (loose associations). His speech is peppered with puns and rhymes, and occasionally with clang associations. David can be re-directed to the question at hand, but inevitably heads off in a tangential manner. He answered questions with considerable elaboration, being overinclusive of detail and providing much extraneous information

Thought Content: David often returned to the theme of things his father had told him, particularly warnings about leaving home and playing the piano. On a number of occasions David expressed the notion that he was being punished or condemned, though this did not appear to be of delusional intensity. He denied having any phobias.

Affect & Mood: David's mood was persistently jovial despite many interruptions in the interview. He enjoys the puns he makes and tries repeatedly to liven up the room and get those around him to join in a form of verbal jousting. He is gregarious and at least moderately disinhibited. He said that he felt very happy to be alive, and that this was his usual mood state. David rated his mood at 8/10.

Perception: David denied having hallucinations or illusions in any sensory modality. He often hears the voice of his father telling him things, but recognizes that he is playing back past events in his mind. He did experience auditory hallucinations of a derogatory, critical nature when he was first ill in England.

Cognitive Functioning: David was largely unable to participate in cognitive testing because he thought it was a game and he would try to change the rules when asked one of the tasks. He was oriented to person, place, and time. He demonstrated intact immediate and short-term memory function. His attention span appeared to be notably limited, but was not able to be formally assessed.

Diagnostic Formulation

David is a fortyish, divorced man who lives in a boarding house. He has a history of serious psychiatric difficulties dating back to his late teens when he had a rapid decompensation while studying in England at the Royal College of Music. He has been institutionalized for much of the time since then, though in recent years he has been able to live in hostels and as a boarder in private homes. He currently presents with an unknown period of disorganization and marginal self care. He requires the support of his landlord for everyday matters. David has a marked thought form abnormality in which he maintains a continuous, pressured dialogue. At times he demonstrates an understandable link between his ideas, at other times this is not evident. While he doesn't currently endorse any delusional thoughts, he has avoided playing the piano – his life's passion – because of memories of his father telling him he'd be punished for leaving the family to pursue his career. David is extremely outgoing and jovial, often inappropriately hugging and kissing strangers. He is quite distractible and has an increased level of activity.

David does not appear to experience perceptual disturbances. He denies any symptoms of depression. There is no evidence that a general medical disorder or substance use has initiated or is maintaining his symptoms. His symptoms, while long-standing, clearly had a prodrome and acute phase which affected him in his late teens.

Preferred/Provisional Diagnosis

Schizoaffective Disorder, Bipolar Type
Possible Neuroleptic-Induced Akathisia

Differential Diagnosis

Schizophrenia, Disorganized Type
Schizophrenia, Undifferentiated Type
Psychotic Disorder Not Otherwise Specified
Mood Disorder Not Otherwise Specified

Etiologic Formulation

	Biological Aspects	Social Aspects	Psychological Aspects
Predisposing Factors	Genetic loading Possible Paranoid Personality Disorder in father	Isolation from family/Refusal of father to allow contact after David left home David's father usually made decisions for the entire family	Strong desire to win competitions and please father Studying with highly acclaimed professor who actually played for Rachmaninoff
Precipitating Factors	Poor sleep and nutrition and the time of the performance	Difficulty in making friends Ostracized/taken advantage of by other students	Stress of the performance and the high expectations placed on him
Perpetuating Factors	Partial response to psycho-pharmacological treatment Possible serious side effects to medication	Lack of vocational skills other than music performance Lack of professional mental health care involvement	Living the self-fulfilling prophecy that his father told him (about leaving home) Guilt about choosing to leave home
Protective Factors	Partial response to psycho-pharmacological treatment, may be able to achieve a better result In good health overall	Able to make friends and interest those around him in providing assistance Able to mesmerize listeners with his playing ability	Open to new ideas and new people in his life Above average intelliigence

Biopsychosocial Management Plan

	Biological Aspects	Social Aspects	Psycho-logical Aspects
Invest-igations	Physical examination Routine hematologic and biochemical screening to see if there are contra-indications for pharmacologic treatment	Information from hospitals in England and Australia Collateral history from family, landlord, etc.	Consider neuropsychiatric evaluation to assess cognitive functioning
Short-Term Treatment	Treat any concurrent physical illness Consider a novel antipsychotic and mood stabilizer	Social Skills Training Assertiveness Training Consider Speech Therapy	Psychoeducation for family and others involved with David Possible Behavior Modification/ Therapy
Longer-Term Treatment	Optimization of medication Health teaching about cigarette smoking	Arrange a case manager Consider Vocational Training Possible return to music performance	Ongoing care with a supportive focus Active Community Treatment

Psychiatric Commentary on 'Shine'

While schizophrenia is increasingly being found to have a genetic cause, a major psychosocial aspect is well illustrated here. A **double bind** is a "damned if you do, damned if you don't" situation. This in and of itself does not cause schizophrenia, but susceptible individuals may withdraw into psychosis to avoid unsolvable conflicts. In this film, David is pushed not only to master difficult musical pieces, but to win competitions. Despite this, his father resists getting him a teacher and ultimately agrees only when someone agrees to provide lessons free of charge. David's father later prohibits him from accepting a scholarship in the U.S. (note: the father as depicted in the film, has a **paranoid personality disorder**). Finally, David's talent earns him another scholarship, and if he is to develop as a musician, it is clear that he must leave. His father vehemently opposes this, saying it will destroy the family. When David insists, his father tells him he cannot return, that he will have no family, and that he will be punished for the rest of his life. David is thus placed on a locomotive-driven track towards a crisis as he leaves. His breakdown into psychosis, months in development, occurs during his performance as he dissociates from reality. Afterwards, he is clearly changed, and doesn't have the capacity to study as intensively as he did before his illness.

What follows is a good depiction of **negative symptoms**. David is markedly inattentive to his surroundings. He is ambivalent about many important matters, living largely in an autistic world of cigarettes, obscure language, and finally, a return to the piano. In one scene, a woman takes him from an institution and offers to drive him to her home. She asks him not to smoke in her car. He obliges, but instead of putting out his cigarette, he walks along side the vehicle and continues smoking. This is an example of **concrete thinking**, where people lose their ability to understand an event in its fuller context and cannot grasp abstract meanings. David relies on the kindness and tolerance of others (e.g. strangers, his landlord) to ensure his safety. All of the above features are consistent with schizophrenia, and in particular, how it develops over time. The peak onset in males is from age 15 to 25, often occurring in the first year or two of post-secondary education. As good a depiction as this is, the portrayal in *Shine* is more consistent with a **schizoaffective disorder** because of David's persistent mood symptoms.

References

Code of Medical Ethics
American Medical Association; Chicago, 1999

Diagnostic and Statistical Manual of Mental Disorders, 4th Ed.
American Psychiatric Association; Washington D.C., 1994

Practice Guidelines for the Treatment of Psychiatric Disorders – Compendium 2000
American Psychiatric Association; Washington D.C., 2000

Introductory Textbook of Psychiatry, 2nd Ed.
N.C. Andreason & D.W. Black
American Psychiatric Press, Inc.; Washington D.C., 1995

Screening Laboratory Evaluation in Psychiatric Patients: A Review
T.J. Anfinson & R.G. Kathol
General Hospital Psychiatry 14: 248 – 257, 1992

Clinical Handbook of Psychotropic Drugs, 10th Ed.
K. Bezchlibnyk-Butler & J. Jeffries
Hogrefe & Huber; Seattle, 2000

Psychiatric Dictionary, 7th Ed.
R. J. Campbell
Oxford University Press; New York, 1996

Psychiatric Secrets
J. Jacobson & A. Jacobson (Editors)
Hanley & Belfus; Philadelphia, 1996

Synopsis of Psychiatry, 8th Ed.
H. Kaplan & B. Sadock (Editors)
Williams & Wilkins; Baltimore, 1998

Notes on Countertransference
O. Kernberg
J. of the American Psychoanalytic Assoc. 13: 38 – 56, 1965

Psychotropic Drugs Fast Facts, 2nd Ed.
J. Maxmen & N. Ward
W.W. Norton & Company; New York, 1995

Interviewing Skills in Relation to Psychiatric Residency
J.R. McCready & E.M. Waring
Canadian Journal of Psychiatry 31: 317 – 322, 1986

Clinical Manual of Psychiatric Diagnosis and Treatment: A Biopsychosocial Approach
R.W. Pies
American Psychiatric Press, Inc.; Washington D.C., 1994

The Use of Laboratory Tests in a Psychiatric Hospital
M.S. Rapp, J.A. Bibr & K. Campbell
Canadian Journal of Psychiatry 37: 137 – 139, 1992

Psychopharmacology of Antidepressants
S.M. Stahl
Martin Dunitz, London, England, 1998

Psychopharmacology of Antipsychotics
S.M. Stahl
Martin Dunitz; London, England, 1999

Psychiatry for Medical Students, 3rd Ed.
R. Waldinger
American Psychiatric Press, Inc.; Washington DC, 1997

Benefits and Problems of Routine Laboratory Investigations in Adult Psychiatric Admissions
A.J. White & B. Barraclough
British Journal of Psychiatry 155: 65 – 72, 1989

Note
The mnemonics for clinical disorders appearing in this book are based on the DSM-IV. Where possible, the actual wording from the diagnostic criteria was incorporated. Used with permission of the American Psychiatric Association.

Recommended Reading

The author has found these titles to be particularly helpful (in addition to those listed in the *References* Section).

Diagnosis/Differential Diagnosis

DSM-IV Made Easy: The Clinician's Guide to Diagnosis
J. Morrison
Guilford Press; New York, 1995

DSM-IV Casebook: A Learning Companion to the Diagnostic and Statistical Manual of Mental Disorders
R.L. Spitzer, M. Gibbon, A.E. Skodol & M.B. First
American Psychiatric Press, Inc.; Washington D.C. 1994

DSM-IV Handbook of Differential Diagnosis
M.B. First, H.A. Pincus & A. Frances
American Psychiatric Press, Inc.; Washington D.C., 1995

DSM-IV Internet Companion
M.R. Morrison & R.F. Stamps
W.W. Norton & Co.; New York, 1998

Child Psychiatry

Do They Grow Out of It? – Long-Term Outcomes of Childhood Disorders
L. Hechtman (Editor)
American Psychiatric Press, Inc.; Washington D.C., 1996

Child and Adolescent Psychiatry
D.X. Parmelee
Mosby; St. Louis, 1996

Consultation-Liaison Psychiatry

Essentials of Consultation-Liaison Psychiatry
J.R. Rundell & M.G. Wise (Editors)
American Psychiatric Press, Inc.; Washington D.C., 1999

Mass. General Hospital Handbook of General Hosp. Psychiatry
N.H. Cassem, T.A. Stern & J.F. Rosenbaum (Editors)
Mosby; St. Louis, 1997

Sigmundoscopy: Medical-Psychiatric Consultation-Liaison
D. J. Robinson
Rapid Psychler Press; Port Huron, Michigan, 1999

Geriatric Psychiatry
American Psychiatric Press Textbook of Geriatric Psychiatry
E.W. Busse & D.G. Blazer (Editors)
American Psychiatric Press, Inc.; Washington, D.C. 1996

Interviewing Skills
The Clinical Interview Using DSM-IV
E. Othmer & S.C. Othmer
American Psychiatric Press Inc.; Washington D.C., 1994

The First Interview: Revised for DSM-IV
J. Morrison
Guilford Press; New York, 1994

Psychiatric Interviewing: The Art of Understanding, 2nd Ed.
S.C. Shea
W. B. Saunders Co.; Philadelphia, 1998

Three Spheres: A Psychiatric Interviewing Primer
D.J. Robinson
Rapid Psychler Press; Port Huron, Michigan, 2000

Medicolegal Issues
Medicolegal Issues in Clinical Practice
D. J. Wear-Finkle
Rapid Psychler Press; Port Huron, Michigan, 2000

Malpractice Risk Management in Psychiatry
F. Flach (Editor)
Hatherleigh Press; New York, 1998

Mental Status Exam
Brain Calipers, 2nd Ed. (in press – due 10/2001)
D.J. Robinson
Rapid Psychler Press; Port Huron, Michigan, 2001

Personality Disorders

Psychoanalytic Diagnosis: Understanding Personality Structure in the Clinical Process
N. McWilliams
Guilford Press; New York, 1994

Disorders of Personality: DSM-IV and Beyond, 2nd Ed.
T. Millon & R. D. Davis
John Wiley & Sons; New York, 1995

Disordered Personalities, 2nd Ed.
D.J. Robinson
Rapid Psychler Press; Port Huron, Michigan, 1999

Psychopharmacology

Handbook of Essential Psychopharmacology
R.W. Pies
American Psychiatric Press, Inc.; Washington D.C., 1998

Essential Psychopharmacology: Neuroscientific Basis and Practical Applications, 2nd Ed.
S.M. Stahl
Cambridge University Press; New York, 2000

Instant Psychopharmacology: A Guide for the Nonmedical Mental Health Professional
R.J. Diamond
W.W. Norton Co.; New York, 1998

The American Psychiatric Press Textbook of Psychopharmacology, 2nd Ed.
A.F. Schatzberg & C.B. Nemeroff (Editors)
American Psychiatric Press, Inc.; Washington D.C., 1998

Psychotherapy

Psychodynamic Psychiatry in Clinical Practice, 3rd Ed.
G.O. Gabbard
American Psychiatric Press, Inc.; Washington D.C., 2000

Doing Brief Psychotherapy
M.F. Basch
Basic Books; New York, 1995

Current Psychotherapies, 5th Ed.
R.J. Corsini & D. Wedding (Editors)
F.E. Peacock Publishers, Inc.; Itasca, Illinois, 1995

Treatment Planning for Psychotherapists
R.B. Makover
American Psychiatric Press Inc.; Washington D.C., 1996

Substance Use Disorders
American Psychiatric Press Textbook of Substance Abuse Treatment, 2nd Ed.
M. Galanter & H.D. Kleber (Editors)
American Psychiatric Press, Inc.; Washington D.C., 1999

The Betty Ford Center Book of Answers: Help for Those Struggling With Substance Abuse and for the People Who Love Them
J.W. West
Pocket Books; New York, 1997

The Craving Brain: The Biobalance Approach to Controlling Addiction
R.A. Ruden & M. Byalick
HarperCollins; New York, 1997

Suicidality
The Practical Art of Suicide Assessment: A Guide for Mental Health Professionals and Substance Abuse Counselors
S.C. Shea
John Wiley & Sons; New York, 1999

The Harvard Medical School Guide to Suicide Assessment and Intervention
D. Jacobs (Editor)
Jossey-Bass; San Francisco, 1999

Index

The Author

Dave Robinson is a psychiatrist practicing in London, Ontario, Canada. His particular interests are consultation-liaison psychiatry, undergraduate and postgraduate education. A graduate of the University of Toronto Medical School, he completed a Residency in Family Practice before entering the Psychiatry Residency Program. He is a Lecturer in the Department of Psychiatry at the University of Western Ontario in London, Canada.

The Artist

Brian Chapman is a resident of Oakville, Ontario, Canada. He was born in Sussex, England and moved to Canada in 1957. His first commercial work took place during W.W. II when he traded drawings for cigarettes while serving in the British Navy. Now retired, Brian was formerly a Creative Director at Mediacom. He continues to freelance and is versatile in a wide range of media. He is a master of the caricature, and his talents are constantly in demand. He doesn't smoke anymore. Brian is an avid trumpeter, and performs regularly in the Toronto area as a member of three bands. He is married to Fanny, a cook, bridge player, and crossword puzzle solver extraordinaire.

Rapid Psychler Press was founded in 1994 with the aim of producing textbooks and resource materials that further the use of humor in mental health education. In addition to textbooks, Rapid Psychler specializes in producing 35mm slides, overhead transparencies, and digital graphics for presentations.

Rapid Psychler Press